Praise for *Cosmic Connection*

"Whether you believe in spirit communication or not, this book offers powerful universal wisdom that can change the way you think about your world."
    —Stephanie Marisca Straight, program director of
    All That Matters, a yoga and holistic education center

"Carole Lynne makes me feel that all of us have the possibility of experiencing greater depth of spirituality. Reading *Cosmic Connection* helps me understand that all of us can connect with Divine Consciousness."
    —Marysia Gensler, Iyengar Yoga instructor

"*How to Get a Good Reading from a Psychic Medium* is an indispensible part of my ongoing research into gifted individuals who are able to connect with those who have crossed over, and *Cosmic Connection* is Carole Lynne's story of her guided journey to accept her gift. It has expanded my understanding and appreciation of what it takes to accept the flow of cosmic energy."
    —Ray Anthony Shepard, author of *Conjure Tales*

"*Cosmic Connection* has come at a monumental time in the evolution of humankind. The Energy will guide each one of us to our own unique creative place on Earth and in the cosmos, both fulfilling our lives and aiding the course of humanity to the realization that we are one. Thank you, Carole Lynne, for reminding us of this basic truth through your work as a psychic medium, minister, and spiritual counselor."
    —Mario A. Aranda, spiritual musician

"Carole Lynne has stepped out of the spiritual closet to bring forward her very personal experiences as a trance channel. Her connection with her Guidance is a much-needed door opener to a deeper understanding of our own experiences. Her story leads you onward, anxious to find out what will happen next. At times, I felt like I was reading a mystery. This book will become a classic within the field of metaphysics."

—Barbara Szafranski, owner of Angelica of the Angels and Angels Landing of Salem, MA

"Carole Lynne in this book has given us a gift—a gift of knowing that we can become a part of the solution and not a part of the problems that our universe is experiencing. That it is up to us to create and maintain our own happiness and that of this great universe. No one has all the answers as to what is beyond, but we understand that the more importance we place on the idea of Oneness, the clearer it becomes that we are all spirit and that the cosmic energy that makes up our being resonates with all others. I could not put this book down; it was absolutely filled with Carole Lynne's beautiful energy and love. Thank you for sharing your spiritual journey with us. I anxiously await the continuation of this wondrous path that we are traveling."

—Rev. Mary Kingslien, pastor at the Church of Spiritual Awakening, Kissimmee, Florida

"As a medical scientist who always questioned how I knew what I knew, information that I had received not from a book, I was reminded by Carole Lynne's *Cosmic Connection* that I was, and am, tuned in to my higher self and divine wisdom. Her book supports trusting this blessing from the universe."

—Sondra Barrett, Ph.D., author of *The Soul of Wine* and co-author of *Radiant Minds: 35 Scientists Explore the Nature of Consciousnes*

Cosmic Connection

Messages for a Better World

Carole Lynne

WEISERBOOKS
San Francisco, CA / Newburyport, MA

First published in 2009 by
Red Wheel/Weiser, LLC
With offices at:
500 Third Street, Suite 230
San Francisco, CA 94107
www.redwheelweiser.com

Library of Congress Cataloging-in-Publication Data

Lynne, Carole.
 Cosmic connection : messages for a better world / Carole Lynne.
   p. cm.
 ISBN 978-1-57863-440-8 (alk. paper)
 1. Lynne, Carole. 2. Women mediums--Biography. 3. Spiritualism. I.
Title.
 BF1283.L96A3 2009
  133.9'1--dc22

                    2008046663

Cover and text design by Donna Linden
Typeset in Perpetua and Requiem
Cover photograph © narvikk/iStockphoto.com

Printed in the United States of America
MV
10 9 8 7 6 5 4 3 2 1

The paper used in this publication meets the minimum requirements of the American
National Standard for Information Sciences—Permanence of Paper for Printed Library
Materials Z39.48-1992 (R1997).

*I dedicate this book to three health practitioners in Newton,
Massachusetts, who have, for over twenty-five years,
taught me to pay attention and be disciplined:*

Jeanne Hubbuch, M.D.
Robert Gensler, D.C.
Paul Duffell, D.D.S.

Contents

Part Three:

The Path Widens 179

A Warning

~~~~~~~~~

THIS BOOK IS NOT INTENDED to take the place of the advice from spiritual directors, doctors, psychologists, or counselors. This is one woman's story of her personal spiritual experience.

Carole Lynne reminds her students and all who read this book that spiritual experiences do not take the place of medical help. If you have physical, emotional, or mental problems that require the help of medical professionals, get the assitance you need. Carole Lynne says: "If you are subject to hallucinations that frighten you because of the negative feelings associated with these experiences, consider your experiences as emotional or mental problems. In my experience, communication with those in spirit and within the higher realms, are positive experiences and do not cause emotional distress."

Introduction:
Message from Carole Lynne

~~~~~~~~~~~~~~~~~~~~

HELLO AND WELCOME INTO MY THOUGHTS, my heart, and my soul. This book is about spiritual experience. As a woman in her sixties who is a wife, mother, grandmother, teacher, Spiritualist minister, psychic medium, writer, musician, and friend to many, I have a story to share with you. As you read it, you will see that Spirit has spoken to me in many ways: through lucid dreams, out-of-body experiences, waking visions, revelations, precognitions, and many inspirational experiences while I was in a light trance state. I have learned a great deal as I have communicated with realms I never imagined existed.

The spiritual experiences I write about in this book are personal, and there is no way to verify them. I am allowing myself to share these unverifiable experiences solely because I have brought much evidence that *is* verifiable by the people I have done readings for. When working as a psychic medium and communicating with a loved one in spirit, most of the evidence is about what the person was like when he or she was alive. Because much of the evidence has been verified, I cannot dismiss all the nonverifiable experiences I have had. The verifiable evidence has proved to me that there is a world of the spirit that we can communicate with.

As you read my story, know that it is an ongoing experience. As a teacher of spirituality and spirit communication, I make it very clear to my students that no matter what I say at any given moment, I may change my mind in the future. I often look at my watch before making a statement and say, "This evening at 8:43 I have a belief that I am about to share with you. However, if I should learn something new that changes my thinking, my belief will change, perhaps by next year or perhaps by tomorrow evening."

I do not want to sound like an authority figure in my classes or in this book just for the sake of being authoritative. The doubts and questions that I have about my spiritual experiences are the same feelings that my students and many readers may have. My conflicts are real and shared by many people. So I am not interested in hiding my vulnerability just to appear like I know what I am doing. My vulnerability *is* my story.

While I am vulnerable as I interact with the world of spirit, I am by no means a pushover. Just because the world of spirit imparts something to me, I do not fall to the ground and shout "halleluiah." Carole Lynne, on the personality level, sometimes questions and disagrees with the teachings that come through during spiritual experience. The part of my consciousness that I name my Greater Self is able to access teachings that my everyday conscious mind either disagrees with or is not ready for. Part of my story is the three-way interaction between my everyday conscious mind, which I call my go-to-the-grocery-store state of consciousness, my Greater Self, and the world of spirit.

I am finally speaking out because all of us need honest dialogue. Because I have been brought up in a culture where "visions of spirit" are usually dismissed as hallucinations, I kept my story to myself for years, as have many of you. We have been brainwashed to disbelieve our spiritual experiences. We have been taught that the only way to have spiritual experiences is through the guidance of a religious authority figure, such as a minister, priest, or guru. This does not mean that we cannot get a great deal out of being part of an organized religion. I am part of the religion of Spiritualism, and I receive a great deal from this religion. However, my story is about my direct communication with Spirit.

Do you use the word *Spirit?* If not, you may prefer a term such as *God, the Divine, Great Spirit, Infinite Spirit, the Creator, Divine Consciousness,* or no name whatsoever. My story is not about naming and labeling. It is a story of spiritual discovery and speaks to anyone from any religious affiliation and to those with no formal affiliation. I am speaking to that part within each one of us that is connected to the One from which we came and to which we shall return.

My story is about direct communication with the cosmic spiritual realms—about being part of spiritual spheres that cannot be seen with the naked eye or measured by any current scientific instruments. My experience embraces the one-on-one, direct, mystical, and incredibly transforming relationship that any one of us can have with the Divine. You may see yourself echoed in the stories of my dreams, visions, and messages from other realms of consciousness. Or, if you do not relate to my story, you may be encouraged to speak with the Divine in your own way.

I perceive the spiritual energy that I communicate with as nothing like a spirit guide or angel. I understand that I am merging with an energy that is intelligent, evolving, and cannot be personified. While there are ultimately no words to describe this energy, the best words that I can find to describe it are *connection, impulse,* and *creative force.*

While I am a psychic medium, this story is not about communications with my loved ones or yours. With all due respect to your loved ones and mine, and with a firm commitment to continue to communicate with their spirits, I also have a passion for communicating with intelligences and energies that have evolved far beyond our human experience.

I have come to believe that you and I communicate on many levels of consciousness. Right now, your mind is focused on the words I have written. But there is another dimension of consciousness that our everyday, logically oriented state of mind is not aware of. I speak of a deeper, broader consciousness, a realm where part of you, part of me, and part of every human being exists. We communicate all the time in this other dimension, perhaps when we are sleeping or in a deep state of meditation. Our spiritual selves are not limited to our physical bodies and can travel into spiritual realms, where we can communicate. As you read this book, allow yourself to go into a deeper state, and I will meet you there. As you read, allow yourself to become the stories you are reading, and perhaps you will find answers; perhaps you will be inspired.

If my story can assist you on your spiritual path, then I will have done what I am here to do in this lifetime. The mysterious energy of the world of spirit will help me give my story to you and then help you use whatever you receive for your highest good and for the good of others. When I first began to walk the spiritual path, all I wanted was to receive guidance from the world of spirit about how I could be more successful, more beautiful, make more money, and be happier. I spoke like I thought a spiritual person should speak, and portrayed the image of what I thought a spiritual person should be. But as the vibrations of the spiritual messages and visions I received began to permeate my consciousness, I started to change. I became more in touch with my Greater Self and felt the love of the Divine.

These days, without trying, I am becoming more accepting of myself. It is ironic. The more I accept myself, the less I need to focus on personal issues. While I used to ask, "What can I do to have more of what I need?" these days I often ask, "What more can I do for those *in* need? What more can I do for our troubled world?" Like most of us, on some days I am more self-centered than on others. With the problems our world faces today, none of us can afford to be as self-centered as we have been.

Evolution is not over! The future of our world depends on our abilities to evolve in a positive way: to let go of our egos, to realize that we are not separate beings, and to evolve to a consciousness that finds poverty, pollution, and war unthinkable. We are responsible for the future. But how can we change in order to have better personal lives and to make better choices for our world?

Each one of us needs to change and to focus less on "me" and more on "we." In my opinion, we can't create a better world unless we evolve spiritually. The cosmic connection is the connection to spiritual realms and it belongs to everyone. As we discover the cosmic connection, we receive and we evolve. Our lives improve. The world is changed.

The spiritual journey I have been on has brought me incredible insights and knowledge. I have opened the channel, and the wisdom is flowing through. My communications with the world of spirit have changed the way that I look at reality. I have come to conclusions about the way the universe was formed and continues to exist. I have thoughts about the ways that you and I are all connected by an incredible spiritual energy: the force of all creation. I have connected with cosmic energies and beings that have changed my way of thinking about us. I have received teachings that are changing the ways I want to live. I offer my story in the hopes that you are inspired to pursue your own spiritual path in order to live a better life and in order to bring greater wisdom to our magnificent but troubled world.

In my book *Consult Your Inner Psychic,* I offered you a process for deepening your own intuitive gifts. In my book *How to Get a Good Reading from a Psychic Medium,* I offered advice on deciding what kind of reading you want and how to find a good reader. In *Heart and Sound,* I offered you affirmations, prayers, and chants to use as part of your spiritual practice. In *Cosmic Connection,* I offer you the opportunity to look at the teachings I have received as I have opened the channel and connected with a universal cosmic force. It will help you translate the language of the world of spirit so that you can understand the many ways that it is speaking to you. I have no monopoly on this channel. It is there for everyone. It is there for you.

At the end of our physical lives, we are all on the way home to the eternal world, and we may take different paths to get there. Ride along with me on my path, and then take whatever is useful to you as you make your own choices and find your own path home.

I appreciate your showing up to receive this story.

Carole Lynne

PART ONE

The Early Years
of Awakening

Chapter 1

Opening the Channel

~~~~~~~~~~~~~~~

ON A NICE DAY IN 1987 I was looking around a bookstore when a book called *Opening to Channel: How to Connect with Your Guide* by Sanaya Roman and Duane Packer seemed to jump into my arms. Intrigued, I bought it, took it home, and sat down to read. That book would change my life forever.

Even though I had never heard the word *channel* as I grew up in the forties and fifties, I had many telepathic communications. But these experiences were all about ESP (extrasensory perception). It never entered my mind that they might have some connection to spiritual life. I just found that knowing things about other people was fun. As a teenager at the National Music Camp in Interlochen, Michigan, I discovered that I could actually hear my friend Peter's thoughts. I found this a little hard to believe, but after it went on for a few weeks, I finally said, "Peter, I know this is a strange thing to tell you, but I think I am hearing your thoughts. Were you just thinking about . . . ?" Peter not only verified that what I heard in my mind was what he had been thinking, but also told me that he had been hearing my thoughts. We were fascinated with our new mind-to-mind communication and constantly tested our ability. I would sit in one part of the camp and send images to Peter, and he would write down what he saw. Then he would send me images.

Coincidence—or perhaps fate—would have it that both Peter and I went to the University of Michigan. There I also met my husband-to-be, Marlowe, who was adamant that Peter and I be tested at the Society for Psychical Research in New York City. Around 1961 or '62 Peter and I showed up at the research center. A man named Doctor Ossi escorted us to two different rooms, which had steel walls. I sat in one room and looked at picture cards that the researchers had given to me. I mentally projected the image I saw on each card, and Peter wrote down what he saw. We then reversed the process.

Our experiment showed that we were communicating telepathically, as our scores were beyond what anyone could accomplish by pure chance. But although we were psychic, we did not have incredible scores. That news was a bit of a bummer, as naturally we wanted to be told our scores were the best ever.

After that experiment, I forgot all about psychic experiences. I was interested in writing songs and singing in Greenwich Village. I arrived on the coffeehouse scene shortly after Bob Dylan was just beginning to become famous. All of us singers and guitarists who played music and passed the basket for tips focused on being discovered by some talent agent, like Dylan had been.

Ten years later I was in Mill Valley, California, part of the San Francisco Bay area. While a famous talent agent had not discovered me, I was blessed with two children. So I was busy being a mom, singing in clubs a few nights a week, and teaching kids and their mothers to play guitar and sing. I had no time to become involved in what I learned, years later, was the "spiritual revolution" of the seventies. Women's liberation certainly got my attention, and I wrote and sang feminist songs in women's coffeehouses in Berkeley. There were times when song lyrics just seemed to pop into my head, as if the music and words had been already written someplace else and were simply being delivered to my brain. When I had those magical songwriting experiences, I did think that perhaps I was in contact with a power greater than myself.

But it was only half a thought. (You know those thoughts that almost form in your mind but are not clear enough for you to recognize as a thought? Those are what I call "half a thought.")

When my dog, Queenie, died in 1980, I saw her spirit walk across my living room. While my vision was very real to me, I did ask myself, "Is this spirit or my imagination?" I had no idea that Queenie was the first of thousands of human and animal spirits that I would see in my lifetime.

In 1980 my husband got a job offer in Boston, and we moved. I continued to play music and take care of my kids. I had been living in the Boston area about seven years when I walked into that bookstore and bought *Opening to Channel*. I had no idea that my whole experience of reality would change and that dimensions I had never heard of or thought about would become part of my regular, day-to-day existence. I would learn that when people and animals die, their spirits live on. I would learn that those of us who are still living on the earth plane could actually communicate with the spirits of our loved ones. I would learn that there is an incredible power, greater than any one of us, and this power is the Energy that created this universe and continues to create it each second. I would learn that this Energy, which many of us call God, Infinite Spirit, Cosmic Consciousness, or the Divine, is the Energy that supports and guides us in our daily lives, if only we would listen.

I learned and I learned. I accepted that I was a medium (a person who can communicate with the spirits of those who have passed on) and started giving spiritual consultations where I brought messages to clients from their loved ones in spirit. I accepted that I was a writer and started writing books. I channeled and I channeled, but for some reason, I did not accept that I *was* a channel. Every day I sat in my basement and recorded cassette after cassette of the words I was hearing in my mind. I spent hours and hours transcribing those tapes. But then I hid the tapes and stuffed all the transcriptions of my channeling sessions into my dresser drawers where no one would read them. "People will think I am crazy," I told myself.

Between 1994 and 2003, I took courses with the American Federation of Spiritualist Churches and received credentials as a medium, healer, and minister. I flew across the ocean and studied at Arthur Findlay College in Stansted, England, where I heard about mediums who did trance work. At this school, I watched mediums go into altered states of consciousness and speak the words that "flowed through them" from the world of spirit. I was totally amazed, because *this was what I had been doing in my basement for years.* I had been going into an altered state of consciousness, asking a question, and speaking the words that I "heard" coming to me from someplace else.

"How do we know these mediums are really connecting with the world of spirit?" I asked my teachers. "How do we know that the wisdom they are bringing through, while wonderful, is not coming from their imagination?" There I sat in Stansted, in one of the most beautiful English courtyards that you will ever see, wondering about the source of the inspirational, life-changing words that flowed effortlessly out of the mouths of the trance mediums.

One day a teacher named Nora Shaw said something in class that transformed my life:

> If a medium can do an evidential reading and bring evidence that she is in touch with your uncle or aunt or another of your loved ones—evidence that she does not have any knowledge of—and therefore prove beyond any doubt that she is communicating with Uncle John in spirit, then it is also quite possible that when this same

medium feels that she is bringing through wisdom from a spiritual source, that she is.

When I heard these words, I said to myself, "I am going to become an evidential medium and prove that I can communicate with the spirits of loved ones who have passed over. And if I can prove to myself and my clients that I can communicate with their grandparents, their parents, sisters, brother, wives, husbands, children, and pets, then and only then will I take those transcriptions of the channeling sessions out of the dresser drawers and share them with the world."

In the years that followed, I proved to myself that I can communicate with the spirits of those who have passed over. In a reading, a person can verify everything I say about his or her grandfather. The person can say, "Yes, my grandfather was involved in a lot of legal battles," or "No, my grandfather did not have a son as you say he did." The person knows the answers and so can verify the evidence. When I tell people that I feel a Divine guidance bringing messages to help them have better relationships with their family, there is no way to verify that I am getting that advice from the Divine or from my mind. But, as Nora Shaw said, because I am able to give evidential readings, it is "quite possible" that when I feel I am bringing wisdom through from a spiritual source, I am.

Since I have proven to myself that I have a link with the world of spirit, I feel justified in sharing my many visions of spirit and messages brought from a higher source of guidance. Some would have shared their visions right away, but I needed proof that I could link with the world of spirit before sharing the experiences of my spiritual journey.

Now that I have that proof, oddly enough, it does not seem as important anymore. Of course, I continue my readings, as many of my clients still need the kind of proof that I needed years ago.

However, I have changed. I now know that there is a part of all of us that survives death. I cannot explain how I know. I just know, and it took me from the time I was born in 1940 until 2008 to "just know."

Spirit Knocks on My Door

Many teachers from various religions and spiritual paths would have been more than happy to tell me how to live my spiritual life and what was to be expected of me. And for many people, the best way to get spiritual direction is from teachers and spiritual leaders. But the mystic personality needs direct communication with the Divine. The mystic personality does not want to be told what to do, but wants to discover the spiritual path through personal experiences with the Divine.

Years ago, I did not realize that the word *mystic* might apply to me. To be honest, I had never thought much about the word and did not really know what it meant. It was a word I associated with spooky people and marketing campaigns for places that wanted to appear to have a spiritual environment. I had heard of the Christian mystics, but always imagined them to be people who went off the deep end. Nobody understood them, and many of them were killed for their spiritual practices. When I heard Sunday school teachers talk about the mystics, it was always with an attitude that said to me, "Learn about these mystics, but do not try this at home." These teachers taught me that the mystics were people who lived long ago, and we do not communicate with God now as they did then. I was taught that mysticism belongs to the past, and we should leave it where it belongs. I guess I did not learn this lesson well enough, because later in life, I was open-minded enough for the world of spirit to get my attention. "Hey you, we are trying to get your attention. We have a job for you."

Once I had opened "the channel" and was receptive to hearing from the world of spirit, I was spoken to in many ways. The Divine led me to the spiritual work that I am doing today as a psychic medium and as a Spiritualist minister and healer. But I also needed to hear from the Divine personally. Over the years I would learn that the Divine has always had to communicate with human beings in mysterious ways, such as dreams, revelations, synchronicities, and the imagination.

Chapter 2

Dreams Reveal in Frankfurt and Paris

~~~~~~~~~~~~~~~~

IN 1991 I WAS WORKING as a public speaking consultant and singing coach. One of the companies I worked for regularly was participating at the International Textiles Manufacturers Association (ITMA) convention in Hanover, Germany, and asked me to come along. My husband and I flew to Frankfurt and checked into the Frankfurt Hotel and Towers. As I went to sleep, I had no idea that a Being from another dimension was going to greet me.

The Man-in-the-Mountain Dream

~~~~~~~~~~~~~~~~

Here are the notes I took upon waking from the dream:

I am flying near a mountainside. The soil is red and dotted with low bushes and trees. The land seems dry but rich. The side of the mountain starts to look different, and I realize that the front of the mountain is not solid. There is a large curtain. I go up to the curtain and through it into a room. The room resembles a doctor's waiting room. There are people sitting in comfortable chairs. Some of them look unhappy. They are breathing through some large inhalators that come from the wall. The inhalators are white. They seem to be made of heavy plastic and have white tubes, which attach them to the wall. The room is pure white. In another part of the room a man sits dressed in a white suit. He has a very pointed head. [The picture I drew of him after I woke from my dream shows that he is also bald.] As I approach him, I realize that he is a special being. I fall to the floor on my knees as I greet him. The floor is not solid. I bob up and down. His assistant hands me a document. When I read it, I realize that it is an oath that reads, "I pledge to be kind to people." The man stands before me and asks me if I am willing to take this pledge. I agree and then read the pledge out loud.

The scene vanishes, and I am flying high in the air. I feel a little scared and realize that I am fully aware of my flying. At the same time, I am aware of my body sleeping in my hotel bed in Germany. I keep flying and look down to see the ocean below me. The wind is blowing and feels quite cold. I am impressed by how real the wind feels against my skin. I realize that part of me is out of my body, flying. I fly within this strange realm a little longer and then will myself back into my body.

I wake up feeling good, knowing that I have had out-of-body dreams before, but this is the most "tangible" dream and the first time I have ever been so aware of both my body in the bed and my body in the dream.

Years later, I would learn that the kind of dream I had is called a lucid dream: a dream where you know you are dreaming.

As I read my notes today, the dream is as vivid to me as it was when I woke that early morning in Germany. I am grateful that I drew a picture of the mountain, the room, the white plastic instruments, and the man. When I want to recall this dream, all I have to do is to look at my notes and drawings, and the dream comes back to me.

I have heard people say that in an earthquake, the ground feels as if it is rolling beneath your feet. That is how this floor in the mountain felt. I knew the man in white was a specialist of some kind, and I also suspected he was a very wise man from another world. But he did not tell me about his credentials or try to teach me anything. When he pulled out the pledge document, a large scroll, his manner was extremely businesslike. It seemed like he asked people every day to take kindness oaths, and my visit seemed to be one of many. When I woke up, I knew that I had taken a real oath in a real place, but where had I been?

Living a Double Life

I did not have a long time to ponder this question, as I had to get dressed and board a train to Hanover, where I joined my colleagues at ITMA. As I walked around the convention floor, which was crowded with businesspeople from all over the world, I felt as if I were in two places at the same time. My physical body was in the convention hall, but another part of me was still in that white room in the middle of a mountain.

Luckily for me, I do not scare easy when it comes to emotional and creative experiences of the mind. I am not much of an adventurer on a physical level: you will not find me hang gliding or parachuting out of airplanes. But mystically, I can cope with a lot. So I was able to adjust quickly to being in two places at once.

This experience on the convention floor was the beginning of my double life. This dream while sleeping was just the teaser, the opening act, if you like. I would go on to have many visions and travel into many different dimensions while I was awake.

My husband had to be at a meeting in Frankfurt nine days after the end of the ITMA convention. Talk about an obvious window for a vacation. We did not feel like hanging around Frankfurt, and we boarded a train that took us to Belgium and on to Paris.

We checked into the Hotel de Notre Dame. It would have been a very posh hotel experience were it not for the fact that our 22-year-old son was street singing in Paris, and he and his buddy needed a place to take a shower every day. Of course we said, "Yes, you are welcome to our hotel room." The floor in our room quickly turned into a tapestry of wet towels, dirty socks, and guitar picks. Until they got busted for singing on the street and left town, our room became a place for them to charge their small amplifiers We escaped our hotel room and wandered the streets of Paris.

Waking Dream in Paris

There is nothing more wonderful than standing outside the Notre Dame Cathedral on a sunny day in October. The sun was warm, but not too warm. My husband went off to have a cup of coffee and a pastry in one of those beautiful Paris coffee shops, and I headed into the cathedral. The beauty of the cathedral and the sound of the organ overwhelmed me. After walking through to the back of the cathedral and back to the door I had entered, I had a sudden impulse to visit the *Crypte Archeologique,* which is housed underneath the Notre Dame grounds. The crypt contains remnants of ancient walls and foundations of cities that existed several hundred years before the cathedral was built.

As I walked along the stone floors of the crypt, I felt myself start to travel into another dimension. I knew my body was in the physical space of the crypt, but I was beginning to feel different. My eyes were drawn to a large stone formation on the other side of the room. From across the room, it looked like another ancient building foundation. I could not tell anything about its history; I just knew that it was calling out to me. As I gazed across this room at it, I suddenly had a vision or a waking dream. A woman appeared to me, and she held children in her arms. She seemed to be protecting these children. I felt a great love pouring from the heart of this woman to these children.

Beside each display in the crypt is a sign that tells the visitor what he or she is looking at. I remember that the sign for this particular stone foundation mentioned Saint Genevieve, the patron saint of Paris. Not being a history buff and not being brought up Catholic, I had never heard of Saint Genevieve. I stood before the sign, wondering if my vision of the woman protecting children had something to do with this saint. While my logical mind tried to make sense of my vision, I began to feel dizzy from the incredible energy I had experienced. I knew I had to get out of the crypt to get some air—and also to get some information about Saint Genevieve.

I grabbed several tourist booklets on the way out of the crypt, but they said nothing about Saint Genevieve except that she was the patron saint of the city. Some books did not even mention her.

Feeling half drunk with the energy that was around me, I stumbled out onto the cathedral courtyard and tried to calm myself. I thanked God that I was by myself when I had this experience, because if I had been with friends or my husband, I knew that I would have shut down and pushed away the vision. I had to be alone in order to see and experience what I saw.

A knowing came over me, and suddenly my eyes were drawn to two men out of the hundreds of people milling around the courtyard. I knew that these men, who were standing about ten feet from me, would have the information I needed in their tourist guidebook. In a normal state of consciousness, I would have felt funny walking up to two strange men in Paris, not even knowing if they spoke English, and asking if I could look up something in their guidebook. But in an altered state of consciousness, and operating in what I would learn years later was another dimension, I found it easy to run up to them and ask politely if I could borrow their guidebook for a few minutes. They did speak English, and in thirty seconds I had the guide in my hands. I looked up Saint Genevieve and found out that she had rescued the children in Paris, saving them from Attila and the Huns. As I read those words, I was astounded. I had seen her, and I had seen the children. I had felt her compassion.

My husband had finished his coffee and pastry and was suddenly in my face, wanting to know how I had enjoyed the cathedral. I said, "It was very nice, dear." One of the things I have learned about traveling into different dimensions and realms is that when someone comes up to you and asks you a question when you are still in another dimension, you snap back suddenly from that other dimension. And when you have just been traveling to another dimension, you cannot always immediately talk about where you have been, even to your loving husband on a beautiful day in Paris.

Two Worlds

~~~

In the Frankfurt dream and the Paris vision, I learned that the seemingly solid and material world was not the only world. I learned that I had more than five senses and that there was a part of me that could travel into different realms and into different periods of time. I also started to suspect that Divine guidance was speaking to me in Its own way.

When I returned to the Boston area, I felt as if I had traveled a lot farther than Europe. I had traveled into different realms and learned about my spiritual path. The oath I took inside the mountain has had more of an effect on my life than any other oath I have ever taken. Experiencing the vision of Saint Genevieve protecting the children of Paris taught me that I could travel back in time.

Comments on My
Frankfurt Dream and Paris Vision

Because I find it beneficial to be open-minded, I've carefully examined what might have been happening during my sleeping and waking visions. The following are several possibilities and my personal conclusions.

Man-in-the-Mountain Dream: Possibilities

Questions: In my man-in-the-mountain dream, did I really enter another world? Did I really meet that man dressed in white, who asked me to take an oath to be kind?

Spiritual Body Traveling to Other Worlds Theory: Many metaphysical teachers say when the physical body is asleep, the astral body can lift itself out of the physical body and travel to anywhere in the universe. In this scenario, my astral body left my physical body, which was laying on the bed in Frankfurt, and traveled to another realm that is not part of the earth plane or any other planet that the scientific world knows of. My astral body flew into the side of the mountain, met with an advanced spiritual teacher, and took an oath to be kind to people.

The Subconscious Theory: In this scenario, both my conscious and subconscious mind were involved with thoughts and feelings about leading a more spiritual life and becoming a kinder person. My subconscious mind created the dream to dramatize my spiritual feelings. Once in the dream state, I had the opportunity to create a meeting with an important spiritual teacher, who had me go through a ritual that included signing an oath to be more kind to people.

Divine Creation Theory: In this case, a part of my mind reached further into the spiritual realm of Divine Consciousness than either my conscious or subconscious mind could reach. My consciousness was able to blend with an energy beyond words and beyond thought. A part of me merged with Divine Consciousness to receive instruction. The man-in-the-mountain dream was the way the Divine impressed on me the need to lead a more spiritual life and to be kind. And in this dream, I was given the opportunity to either sign the oath or not. As I signed it, I made a commitment to the Divine. In this case, the man in the mountain was a creative expression of the Divine.

My Conclusion: I believe that either my spiritual body actually traveled to another realm and I met with an actual spiritual teacher, or that my dream was the Divine's way of bringing me a message and an opportunity to take a spiritual oath. I do not feel that my dream was simply a creation of my subconscious mind. There was a time in my life when I would have scoffed at any theory except the subconscious theory. But after communicating with so many spirits in my work as a psychic medium, I can no longer push away the possibility that I was really in another spiritual realm. I am open to the idea that there are realms within the universe that we do not yet have the scientific resources to explore.

Vision of Saint Genevieve: Possibilities

Question: What really happened when I saw a vision of Saint Genevieve?

The Psychometric Theory: A person is said to be practicing psychometry when he or she is able to obtain information from the energy of a material object. For instance, a psychic holds a watch that belonged to a client's grandfather and, by reading the energy around the watch, is able to tell the client that her grandfather was a general in the army.

If, when I saw the vision of Saint Genevieve, I was unknowingly practicing psychometry, I read the energy around the ancient building foundation that I was looking at while standing in the crypt of Notre Dame. And as I read that energy, I learned that those foundation stones related to a woman and some children. This knowledge would then have formed into a vision of a woman and children. It is important to note that when I had the vision of a woman and several children, I had no idea who they were. Only upon walking across the crypt and reading the sign posted near the foundation did I find the name of Saint Genevieve. It was this sign that made me feel that perhaps the vision of the woman I saw was Saint Genevieve. The psychometric theory says that I did not actually see the *spirit* of Saint Genevieve, but simply obtained information about her from the energy surrounding the foundation and created a picture of her in my mind in response.

The Mediumistic Theory: In this scenario, I saw a vision of a woman and several children, in that moment, in the same way that I now see visions of the spirits of grandparents, parents, spouses, children, and friends of my clients. In this case, I was not reliving a past memory, but communicating in the present with the spirit of someone who had passed into eternal life. I would have had a vision of a woman and several children, and then, upon reading the name of Saint Genevieve on the sign near the foundation, come to the conclusion that the vision I had was most likely a vision of the *spirit* of Saint Genevieve. Then, upon reading more about Saint Genevieve in the guidebook I borrowed, I would have assumed that the children in my vision were those that Saint Genevieve rescued from the forthcoming battle with Attila and the Huns.

The Psychic Theory: In this scenario, I knew psychically what the sign near the rock foundation said. Although I was standing across the room and could not see the sign's words with my physical eyes, I saw them psychically. This psychic information then stimulated my subconscious mind to form the vision of Saint Genevieve and the children. In this case, the children would have been another bit of psychic information, as the sign did not say anything about them.

The Good-Guess Theory: In this theory, I would have simply stood across the room from the rock foundation and guessed correctly that the sign would have the name of Saint Genevieve inscribed on it.

My Conclusion: Many skeptics think that every time a psychic or a medium brings correct evidence, he or she simply made a good guess. But I find it impossible to believe my vision is the result of a good guess. First of all, before that day in the crypt, I had never heard of Saint Genevieve, or if I had, her name was certainly not part of my conscious thoughts at this time. And even if her name was somehow in my subconscious mind, there were many exhibits in the crypt, and I would have not only had to guess that her name was associated with one of the exhibits, but also identify the correct exhibit by guessing.

I can believe that I read the words on the sign with my psychic abilities, as I am psychic. But I am more inclined to feel that I got the information either by psychometrically reading the energy of the foundation and the sign, or by having an actual vision of the spirit of Saint Genevieve. When I first had this experience, it was so emotionally charged that I was sure that I had an actual vision of this saint. In 2008, I am open to the idea that it was not a medium-istic vision of the saint, but a vision I had by reading the energy of the foundation. I have had many psychometric experiences; I have obtained much information from holding objects that belonged to people before they died and by visiting old houses and learning about their histories by reading the energy from the walls.

Looking Back

This trip changed my life forever. Reality would never look the same to me again. Suddenly my world opened up. The reality of the day-to-day life I led seemed to be a small fraction of the whole reality that was available to me. Of course, the logical part of my mind did not want to accept what happened. But as I be-gan to get more in touch with the whole of who I am and how I connect with Divine Consciousness, I realized that my logical mind is only one tool of many that the whole of me contains. Today, when I hear comments from skeptics and atheists, I am not alarmed or angry. I simply feel that the skeptics are missing out on a lot by insisting that everything be measurable by the tools they deem important. To dismiss spiritual experiences and realms because we do not yet have the scientific tools to measure them is like dismissing love, truth, beauty, and God.

As spiritual seekers, we need to investigate our experiences. When you have an important dream, write it down as soon as you can, or keep a tape recorder by your bed so that you can record a description of your dream. Many on the spiritual path either exaggerate or negate their experiences as time passes. None of us wants to be guilty of taking a small incident that happened ten years ago and exaggerating it into a story that is simply not true. We have all heard the fish story that Uncle Charlie tells; somehow, each year, the fish he caught gets larger and larger. On the other hand, we do not want to dismiss important spiritual experiences just because, as time passes, they become too hard to believe. I have had experiences that I started to disbelieve three years later. That is when I get out the notes that I wrote at the time of the experience so I can find out what really happened.

As spiritual seekers, let's all become good detectives—taking notes, drawing pictures, and taking photographs of the events in our lives that have spiritual significance, so the truth about what we experienced will remain in those notes forever.

Sometimes when I doubt that I really had a dream like the man-in-the-mountain dream, all I have to do is open my notebook and read about my experience. Because I took notes and drew pictures of both the dream and the vision of Saint Genevieve, today I am able to look back and remember these visions more clearly. And when I want to tell someone I know a story about something incredible that happened to me, I check my notes first to make sure that I am not starting to tell a big-fish story.

Chapter 3

Kapulpulpik and the Essence of Essence

~~~~~~~~~~~~~~~~~~~~~~

MY OUT-OF-BODY VISIT to the realm of Kapulpulpik is one of the most unusual, puzzling, and thought-provoking experiences I have had on the spiritual path, and it has been extremely hard for me to accept, as it goes against all the common sense my rational mind depends on. I have scoffed at accounts of people who believe that they are originally from other dimensions or from other planets. But if we can communicate with loved ones who have passed over, I acknowledge that other life-forms, other spiritual forms, and other realms may also exist in the universe.

First Mention of Kapulpulpik

~~~~~~~~~~~~~~~~~~

I first started hearing the word *Kapulpulpik* in a number of channeling sessions between September 17 and September 23, 1991, about a week before the trip to Germany and France during which I had the man-in-the-mountain dream and vision of Saint Genevieve. The important and more extensive sessions about Kapulpulpik would not occur until March and April of 1992.

In September 1991, I was still in the early stages of my channeling sessions. The big job in those days was to cope with the intensity of the energy that flowed through me as I went into an altered state of consciousness. It was as if the world of spirit were trying to rewire me so that I could absorb and hold the abundance of energy. I was dizzy and disoriented, and sometimes I was scared. The words were coming too fast and became garbled sentences that I could not understand.

Here is an excerpt from my September 17, 1991, session:

We are many from Cretion longings
>Once you were there
>We roll and tumble
>You are one of us from long ago.
>Cretion was a planet billions of eons away. Kapul . . . Kappul . . . kapulpulpik . . . kappal something, Cretion . . . .

And here is an excerpt from September 23, 1991:

The beginning of time was fusion of interstellar gasses into cretans and clavicks.
>You see into the nucleus of Kapulpulpik.
>This is very old wisdom.

These words confused me, as they were words I had never heard. To this day, I still do not know if I articulated the words properly. Was I using the correct spelling for Kapulpulpik and Cretion? As these words came to me during a channeling session, I was speaking them out loud and then later writing them down as I listened to the recording of the session. When I looked up *Kapulpulpik* in numerous dictionaries, I could not find it or any word close to it. Was I unable to find it because the spelling was wrong? Or was it a word too old to have ever been recorded in a dictionary? And was I spelling the word *Cretion* correctly? Should it have been spelled Cretian or Creatian? The answers to these questions are still a mystery. I had so many questions; what was Kapulpulpik, and what did it mean to see into the nucleus of it?

My Visit to a Cosmic Realm

On March 4, 1992, I learned a lot more about Kapulpulpik and saw it as a sphere. In that day's channeling session, the story "The Essence of Essence" came through and had a profound effect on me.

I ask you to quiet yourself before reading this story and to open your mind to the experience; create an opening on the soul level, so that you can feel the vibration that fills these words. Ask the Guidance that surrounds you for an open heart. The words of this story are mere words, but the real meaning is contained in the vibration *of* the words.

The session begins as I speak about what I am experiencing. The phrase "Carole Lynne still in her own voice" means I spoke the words that follow when I was still in a light enough state to speak in my own voice. As my remarks continue, I went into a more and more altered state of consciousness. The words that follow "My Guidance" are those that I heard in my mind when in a deep altered state. I repeated these words as they came through me. (Words in parentheses are explanations for the reader and are not part of the original session transcript.)

The following is a partial transcript of a March 4, 1992, channeling session.

CAROLE LYNNE STILL IN HER OWN VOICE: It is 7:15 in the evening. In this session I am sitting in the computer chair, and I am using raw moldavite in my left hand and a smooth hematite stone in my right hand. I request my highest guide. I accept no other than the highest guidance for myself and for others. I am going to turn off the tape and meditate for a few minutes before starting the session.

(Pause in session)

CAROLE LYNNE STILL IN HER OWN VOICE: As I am meditating, I see myself flying through the universe—flying among the stars, around the planets. And as I take this journey of imagination, I notice that I smell different aromas that are not normally part of this room that I am sitting in. I remember having this sensation of different aromas in other meditations and suddenly feeling, "What was that? What was that aroma? I don't recognize that aroma. It is nothing I have ever smelled before, very pleasant, slightly sweet, but not overly so."

(Silence for a minute while meditation goes on)

CAROLE LYNNE STILL IN HER OWN VOICE: An awareness is starting of that part of me that does not exist on the earth plane. I feel a deepening of the energy as I begin to reach into the other levels of my experience and my existence that I am not normally conscious of. My body is becoming very still. And now I feel the energy starting to fill me. I am slightly amused by the fact that I am reporting all of this to you as it is happening to me. It is because I am from a background full of broadcasters: born to parents who are disc jockeys and radio announcers, brought up in a tradition of the reporter who must report all that is happening no matter how difficult it is to be in the middle of an experience and reporting it at the same time.

So it is my goal to be able to report to you all that I experience in hopes to take you there with me or to help you find the rest of your existence, which may be similar or different than mine.

I have a vision now of my astral body floating in space. It is a peaceful flight.

I request now my highest guides to speak through me.

I finish my remarks and now start to count myself down into a deeper state. In this session I count from ten to one.

MY GUIDANCE: Good afternoon or good evening, depending on where you may be.

I wish to tell you today of a story of long before One was,
A story of the Essence of Essence.
What do you suppose a raindrop is composed of?
Do not give me your scientific explanation because that is not what we are here for today.

What do you suppose a raindrop is composed of?
It is composed of the vibrations of the violin
The teardrops of a robin
The parts of an old car
The sound of a baby crying
The judge banging his gavel
A spaceship soaring from another planet
The beings you do not see or hear.

What do you suppose a raindrop is composed of?
Nothing and Everything all at the same time.

And if you could take that raindrop and fold it inside itself
and then pull it backwards and forwards
and stretch it and shape it
and pull it into every configuration that your soul could imagine
You would see All That There Is to see.

Kalpulpulpik and the Essence of Essence

Essence wanted to dream.

Essence, being nowhere and everywhere at the same time, wanted to have some visible locations.

Essence wanted the creative challenge of being something, even though it knew in all its wisdom that it would always be what it was in the beginning.

The heart of Essence began to cry and laugh and share all the joys and sorrows.

And as the vibrations began to plump up a bit, they began to spread.

And soon they were calling out to each other

and forming many circles and triangles and squares and hexagrams

and all other such shapes as it fancied itself.

But how can there be a play, if all the players know all the parts, all the time?

It is no learning if One has all the answers at all times.

Ah yes, the answer will remain in the heart of Essence.

But how much more creative and imaginative it would be if all the players did not know all the answers, all the time,

and found themselves in a situation where they could find their pathways home,

and each would find a different pathway,

and Essence would find a hundred thousand, a million, a trillion, a billion souls' answers to finding the way home.

That would be so much more fun

so much more creative

so much more inventive than All Souls having all the answers already.

And so Essence decided that Part of Itself might forget, momentarily, to allow for creativity and imagination to develop to its fullest extent.

Kapulpulpik
  The looking
  The knowing
  The dynamic of exploration
  The feeling of one's way
  The intuitive probe
  The tingling sensation that tells One you are on the path.

"No day at the beach," you say.
  "No easy job," you groan.
  "Hard times are a comin'," you cry.
  "Oh, what a pity
  What a mess
  How will we ever make it work?"
  Oh, the suffering
  The drama
  The excuses
  The procrastinations
  The harboring
  The cheating
  The planning
  The scrutinizing
  The justifying
  The intellectualizing
  The searing
  The sneering
  The tearing apart
  The knifing
  The murdering
  The killing
  The shooting
  All the dynamics of frustration.

Kalpulpulpik and the Essence of Essence

Having forgotten, the frustration spreads like a virus,
    And the virus envelops the planet with morbidity and deprecation.

You who would remember Essence
    will find it easy by opening your heart
    to the sounds
    and the colors
    and the vibrations of ecstasy.
    You will remember, and then you will feel the love that
Essence brings you.
    And that love will flow from you to others on your planet.

It is hard to kill One while singing a lullaby.
    It is hard to destroy while painting a picture.
    It is hard to murder while dancing.

Comments

Each of us sees the world from the personality level that we have created in this lifetime. It is as if each one of us has donned different glasses; each of us has our own special lenses through which we see the world. Therefore, you have reacted to the story of the Essence of Essence from your own viewpoint and state of consciousness.

When I read the story of the Essence of Essence in 1992, shortly after the words flowed from my mouth, I reacted with great emotion. I remember feeling as if I had gone out of my body and visited another realm. I felt very excited and overwhelmed by the experience. As I read the story today, the higher part of my consciousness takes in the vibrations that the story holds. The words contain energies that I can feel within my body. Perhaps you would like to read the story once more and try to feel the energies that are contained within or behind the words.

My Guidance begins, "I want to tell you a story of long before One was." "Before One was" implies that this story goes back to before anything exists in the universe.

The story begins with a question: "What do you suppose a raindrop is composed of?" We learn that just about anything we can think of or imagine is part of a single raindrop: the vibrations of a violin, a robin's teardrops, and parts of an old car. The next section asks the question again: "What do you suppose a raindrop is composed of?" This time we are given a very clear answer: "Nothing and Everything all at the same time." So now we have an image of a raindrop that contains Nothing and Everything.

As the story continues, it is suggested that if we could take this raindrop and fold it inside of itself and pull it in different ways, we would see that everything possible is right inside this incredible raindrop. Suddenly, the raindrop is seen as having its own existence. We can see this raindrop as the only thing that exists before the universe has been created. I imagine this raindrop not as an earthly drop of water, but a drop that contains all the energy of the entire universe. It is the source of all power, energy, and vibration.

The line "Essence wanted to dream" tells us that Essence *is* the energy of creation. This Essence is presented as a raindrop that contains "All That There Is to see."

We understand that Essence is restless; perhaps bored with being a raindrop that contains the energy of the entire universe, hanging in nothingness and everythingness. At the moment, there is no movement outside of that raindrop. While there may be great movement and power within the raindrop, this energy and power is contained. Essence does not want to be contained. Essence wants to let that energy burst out and form the universe.

Essence knows that with the coming of creation, Essence will learn and evolve. Essence knows that as planets are created and as beings who can live on the planets are created, these beings will learn and become smarter as they confront the problems of life. And because Essence *is* the energy of all that has been created, Essence will also learn. Learning is the *only* way for Essence to evolve. There is nothing more to be gained by keeping all the energy of existence cooped up in a single raindrop.

Essence also realizes that as life is created and Essence lets go of a part of itself to become visible in the universe, that part will become living beings and the planets where the beings live. In order for Essence to learn, these beings must not immediately remember that they are part of Essence. Instead, they must use experience and struggle to learn who they are and where they came from. However, a small part of each being will know the truth of its existence and will yearn to go home to the Source of the Energy. And so all those who live will find different ways to evolve and grow spiritually.

As the life of each being ends and each being returns back to the Source, Essence will receive another teaching and will grow stronger and wiser. Essence has thrown its energy out into the universe with a yearning to learn and then come home. This gesture on the part of Essence has given birth to creativity and imagination. The players will find many ways to get home, because each soul will have to find a unique path home. This way of learning is much more fun and creative for Essence than if Essence had given them all a map on how to get home. Essence will learn from each of these souls, and as Essence evolves, so will the universe.

Our story takes a turn, and we are introduced to Kapulpulpik. But what is it? It is not a place or a person, but a dynamic of exploration—an intuitive probe. We are told that a tingling sensation tells One that you are on the path. The dynamic of Kapulpulpik is inviting and positive. As we read about it, we can yearn to be part of this dynamic as it is clearly part of Essence. It is clearly part of the path that leads to spiritual evolution.

Just when we are feeling happy and contemplating the ecstasy that we may find in the dynamic of Kapulpulpik, our story shows us another aspect of all that exists: the dynamics of the less glamorous and more difficult. We are reminded of our daily complaints: we suffer as we make excuses, procrastinate, and groan about the hard times. We busy ourselves cheating, planning, scrutinizing, intellectualizing, and sneering. We live our lives murdering, killing, knifing, and shooting. As we read these words, many of us are saddened by what is happening to our lives and on our planet. We, as part of Essence, started as beautiful energy so full of hope. This energy became planets, living beings, and material things, and now we are creating a real mess.

As we read about the "knifing, murdering, killing, and shooting," some of us may want to cry out, "I am not killing anyone. I am not cheating anyone." But as we look into the depth of our souls, we can see that we live in a world where cheating and murder takes place. We have to ask ourselves, "If we are all connected, are we all responsible?" We think back to the time when All That Is was contained in a single raindrop. We know that before Essence created the universe, the energy of Everything That Exists in the universe was connected and contained. It is clear that Everything in the Universe is still connected but is no longer contained in a single raindrop. What has changed is that Essence, "wanting to have some visible locations," has created the universe, which each one of us is part of. And as part of the universe, we are all connected. We are not separate from Essence, as we are part of Essence. Therefore, we are responsible for all that happens in the universe.

Kalpulpulpik and the Essence of Essence

The idea that we may be ruining our existence is heartbreaking. Have we forgotten too much? Was it a mistake for Essence to create living beings and then make sure that we forgot that we were part of Essence? While we have realized Essence did so in order that we could through struggle learn to cope with existence, has Essence gone too far? Would it have been better for the universe if we had not forgotten our source?

As we read on, the story gives us the answer to these troubling questions: Those of us who will remember Essence will be able to bring the vibrations of love to everything that has been created. All we have to do is open our hearts to the sounds, colors, and vibrations of ecstasy; we are guided to realize that creativity, which *is* the Essence of Essence, is the answer. It is through creativity that we can remember who we are and that we are born *of* Essence, because Essence *is* creativity. As we allow the creative energy to flow through us, we will be absorbed, and we will not be drawn to destruction any longer. Creativity and imagination are the tools of survival. They always have been, and they always will be. We must use these powerful tools for good instead of evil. That is our challenge as living beings.

It is hard to kill One while singing a lullaby
It is hard to destroy while painting a picture
It is hard to murder while dancing

Suddenly we see the word *One* again. We are quickly taken back to the beginning of the story: "A story of long before One was." *One* is that which Essence has created. Everything that has been created is *One*.

The first line, "It is hard to kill One while singing a lullaby," means that we can destroy that which Essence has created. When Essence contained Nothing and Everything within that single raindrop, Essence was still in complete control. But as Essence was both bored and longing to evolve through learning, Essence had to let go of the energy and create the universe. And so Essence created One. Because we are what Essence has created, we are One. While we can live our lives and return to Essence, Essence is no longer in complete control of that which has been created. Each of us is responsible for taking care of One. Each one of us is responsible for taking care of that which has been created: the planets and the living beings.

We are the keepers of the universe now and must use our creativity for good. For example, if we have, with our science, created cars that run on fuel that pollutes our universe and causes a global warming that threatens the existence of the planet earth, then we must use our creativity to create scientific methods of cleaning up the atmosphere. We must use our creativity to develop ways of living that are healthy for us as living beings and healthy for the planet earth. It all depends on us. *That* is a scary thought.

It is clear that as living beings we have a serious responsibility. Essence will support us, as Essence has created us; however, what we become will go back into the energy of Essence, and so Essence will learn the lessons that we have learned.

Wow, what a huge thought: Essence created this universe, but it is now up to those who live to make Essence wiser or less wise. This thought brings the word *God* to mind again as a synonym for Essence. While I have always thought of God as having all the control and being an all-powerful, constant energy, I now see the possibility that all creation is part of God, and therefore our actions form what God becomes. This is a provocative and sobering thought, and it brings many heavy questions to mind:

Is it possible that the nature of God changes and evolves as that part of God that has been created as the universe changes and evolves?

Is it possible that living beings contribute to the evolution of God, as we are part of God?

Is it possible that as we evolve in a positive way, the power of God evolves in a positive way, and that as we evolve in a negative way, the power of God evolves in a negative way?

These thoughts lead to the possibility that the spiritual evolution of the universe is a collaborative project between God and that which has been created.

Many of us would like to believe that Essence, whom we call God, is an all-powerful protector. We would like to believe that God is the parent who can teach us and save us from all harm. But the story of the Essence of Essence leads us to ask, "When God created us, were we not only given free will, but also part of the responsibility for the universe? Is it possible that, at this point, we have the power to destroy our lives and the planet earth? Are we, as a community of living beings, more powerful than we could have ever imagined?"

And what about the evolution of the universe and the evolution of the Essence of Essence? Perhaps the truth is that as we become creative, we will learn, and as we learn, we will remember how to find our way home. And each one of us will find a different path home and bring knowledge back with us, so that the next time a human being is born out of Essence, that human being will become even wiser. As Essence becomes wiser, all of existence evolves and becomes wiser.

As we think about how it feels to sing, create art, and dance, it is hard for us to imagine being destructive and hateful. Creativity has its own special dynamic, which seems opposed to the dynamic of murder. It is hard to imagine both going on at the same time.

Our story tells us:

Kapulpulpik
>The looking
>The knowing
>The dynamic of exploration
>The feeling of one's way
>The intuitive probe
>The tingling sensation that tells One you are on the path

As we read these lines again, we realize that it is the dynamic of Kapulpulpik that we need to absorb, cultivate, find within ourselves, and evolve in order to participate. We need the energy of this dynamic to find the path of exploration. Is perhaps Kapulpulpik the exploration itself? Is it possible that as we enter this dynamic, it becomes part of us and we become a part of it? Is it possible that we become exploration itself? Is it possible that as we merge with Kapulpulpik, we become the dynamic of learning? Is it possible that this dynamic is the Essence of becoming— the essence of evolution itself?

Chapter 4

A Past-Life Agnostic

PAST LIVES—TRUE OR FALSE? I am agnostic about past lives. I do not believe, and I do not disbelieve. I have often had a terrible reaction to people and groups who claim to have had past lives. I have shouted, "People have enough problems to solve in *this* life, so why do they want to start trying to cope with more problems from some supposed past life? Why do people imagine past lives to try to explain away problems in this life and to find someone to blame for current difficulties? It may be easier to blame a past-life experience than to take responsibility in this life!" Many of my friends and colleagues in the spiritual circles I have attended believe in past lives, and so it has been awkward for me to say that I am a past-life agnostic.

I also have friends who grew up in countries where a belief in reincarnation is a part of most people's cultural beliefs. For instance, I travel to India, where Raja, a good friend of my daughter-in-law, took me sightseeing. Raja is Hindu, and as he talks to me about reincarnation, I can see how comfortable he is with his beliefs. As he speaks about his beliefs, I feel enchanted. I long to fully understand what Raja feels, because I can see that a belief in reincarnation makes life all the more worth living. You have a feeling that whatever you do not learn in this lifetime, you will have another chance to learn. And you can be comforted with the idea that when this life is over, there is another life to follow.

I also have a friend who grew up in Cambodia, where reincarnation is easily accepted. When she shared her story about her family's experiences with reincarnation, I asked her if I could interview her. She agreed but requested that I keep her identity private. I shall call her "Friend."

FRIEND: This is the story of my mother's brother. My mom had four siblings: two girls and two boys. And the youngest brother, when he was three years old, he got a fever and died. When he died, he was reborn into another family. He was reborn to a lady one town over from where my mom lived.

CAROLE LYNNE: How did you know this?

FRIEND: When I was growing up, my mom told me.

CAROLE LYNNE: How did your mom find out?

FRIEND: She found out when the boy remembered where he has lived in a previous life. When he was about four years old, he kept telling his mother to take him to his "mother's house." And his mother kept telling him, "I am your mother, and this is your house." But the little boy would answer, "No, I want to go to the other house."

And so his current mother asked the little boy, "Where is this other house?" The little boy was able to direct his mother down the road to his "other house," which was the house my mom grew up in—the house of my grandmother.

The little boy and his mother came into my grandmother's house where my mom had grown up. The little boy said, "This is my house." He and his mother were welcomed into the house, and the little boy crawled up the stairs and went to the exact place on the floor where he had slept in a previous lifetime, when he was the little brother of my mother. Then the little boy said, "I have toys, and here is where I put my toys." And then the little boy went to the exact place where the little brother of my mother had kept his toys.

The families became close, and as the little boy grew up, he was allowed to visit with his family from a previous life. As I grew up, he was considered to be my uncle, even though in this current lifetime we were not blood relatives. To this day our families are still close.

I thanked my friend for sharing this story with me. For her and for the millions of other people whose cultures have believed in reincarnation for generations, this story is not amazing, but familiar. Her story made me feel more comfortable with the concept of reincarnation. While I have read books on the subject, hearing a family story made more of an impression on me than any book I have read on the subject.

Asking My Guidance about Reincarnation and Other Realms

I admit that I need to be more open to the concept of reincarnation. As I have become comfortable channeling and asking questions of the Energy I call "My Guidance," I have asked questions about past lives, and it is obvious to me that My Guidance is teaching me about reincarnation. One might wonder why I am not a total believer if I am receiving spiritual messages about past lives. The fact is that I am the kind of person that needs certain kinds of proof, and so I will keep praying for the proof I need. I need some kind of information about past lives that I can personally verify. I have had so much personal proof that our spirits survive our physical deaths, but I am still waiting for some kind of personal experience that will prove to me beyond a doubt that we do live more than once.

In the meantime, I wish to share the teachings of My Guidance on reincarnation. The messages that have come through teach us that in each lifetime, we have different things to learn. Each of us needs to become comfortable with ourselves and live the lives we have chosen. We are not meant to be like each other.

The following is a partial transcript of a channeling session from April 15, 1992. Many intriguing teachings emerge about past lives, the soul's commission, and our relationship to other universal realms. In my early years of channeling, I was in a light enough trance state to be able to go in and out of the altered state. In this session I interact with My Guidance, asking a question in my own voice, and then going into a deeper state to receive the answer.

CAROLE LYNNE IN HER OWN VOICE: My Guidance, this morning I am feeling a need to understand more about past lives. I know you have said to me that "many lives and many times make delightful rhymes." I have had several books come to me about past lives, and it has been a little upsetting to me. I would like to ask for your guidance in exploring this subject.

(I count myself down into a light trance state.)

MY GUIDANCE: Shells from the sea can tell the story to you better than I can. Walk along the beach, feel the sands of time beneath your feet, and the fantasies that come to you may be true.

Many lives and many times make delightful rhymes. There are many wonderful things that have happened in your past lives.

Do not be afraid by reading all the horror stories of people's past lives. You are only reading one part of the picture.

A Past-Life Agnostic

Rumpelstiltskin and dolls take you back to the time when you were born. Stubborn you were for survival in this world. Others in your condition would have said, "Forget it." But you did survive despite the fears of all around you.

Turn off the tape and allow yourself to sit for a moment and go back farther before your birth.

(I turn off the tape recorder and sit for a while. When I begin to have a vision, I turn on the tape recorder again and describe what I see, as if I were a reporter.)

CAROLE LYNNE IN HER OWN VOICE: I see fear and anger around me. I see myself before my birth as a baby growing inside my mother, and I see lots of anger from my grandmother in California. Lots of fear— a sort of stunned quality in my father but an excitement. Perhaps I have known my father before the life I am about to come into, and perhaps there is a reason why I am coming into his life again.

Yes, I will turn off the tape and go back further, before conception.

(I turn off the tape again, sit for a while, and once in a deeper state, describe what I see.)

CAROLE LYNNE IN HER OWN VOICE: I see myself in another plane of reality. Many beings of light, of slight forms of another realm. This other realm is where I have spent most of my existence. Perhaps there is another reality that I have had . . . what we might call a life on. Not particularly a planet but a dimension. And there is now talk of my going to the earth plane where I have been a couple of times but not many, many times.

Now I see myself flying over the land of Kapulpulpik that I saw in my dream. It is not so much a planet as a dimension, and the colors that I see and the land are not solid. The colors are from the energy of the coming into being, of the creativity, of the imagination. It is the essence of imagination, this place. And in this existence I am connecting with the imagination of those in many different spheres, many different planets, many different worlds. It is almost like this place is the source where some of the imaginative experiences come from.

This place is so vivid as I talk of it, I am starting to perspire profusely, and I have to take off a layer of clothes to even finish this session. For some reason, it seems to me that I have had this reaction before when I have gone to this place in my mind.

And as I am there right now, I also feel my presence in this room. It feels like I need to go to this place and be there regularly to refuel myself, in a sense, because the earth is very uncomfortable to me. It is not at all what I am used to, and yet I am here for a direct purpose: to fuel the imagination of others. And one way that I can be more comfortable here is to allow myself my connection with my homeland, and to understand my purpose and to feel comfortable with it.

My Guidance, do you wish to say something?

MY GUIDANCE: Glorious is the acceptance of the essence of your being.

All fear and discomfort come from separation from this essence.

You are not of the earth. You are right, although you have dabbled in it here and there.

Allow yourself your universal fantasies and your roaming into other spheres. That is what will give you your strength in this lifetime.

It does not matter if you are famous or worldwide.

You are right, that is not your soul's commission.

Those that you are feeding are feeding others, and so it spreads, and a wonderful envelope fills and spreads its message across the universe.

Rest and enjoy the deep rest that you deserve and that you need in order to carry out your soul's commission.

A Past-Life Agnostic

For this deep rest and this deep peace is contagious. And those around you will pick it up from the very vibrations that you are emitting.

You do not need to do a great deal. Put your creativity together and share these with the world in a new way. And people will feel the peace and joy better there.

Those who do not want it may not be ready for it. For it may not be part of their soul's commission to even enjoy that at this time. Do not worry about those who reject you.

CAROLE LYNNE IN HER OWN VOICE: This feels like an important session. You were speaking to me about not having to do very much.

(I need to count myself down again into a light trance state.)

MY GUIDANCE: You are ready for a transformation on earth now. There is no longer a need for the hectic-ness.

And when those around you are involved in it, you must be understanding without being the least bit patronizing. They are not in the same space you are in at this time.

It does not mean that you are superior. It simply means that you are in a different phase of completing your soul's commission.

You have as much to learn from them as they do from you, but it will start to look different on the outside now because you are here to be a teacher and a model, and so your serenity and your peace must show.

Others may have taught in other lifetimes or in a different way.

And so it is not for you to decide that you are some super being, because you are not.

You are here to learn this quality as much as you are here to teach it. And in teaching it, you learn it, and in learning it, you teach it.

Continue as you have.

Refine the colors of your house and the space.

Be comfortable.

Be comfortable in your physical body.

Be comfortable in your physical surroundings.

You know they are only temporary now. So enjoy them while you have them.

But know that they are only housing for a much deeper you.

That is your existence—that is your soul, that is your essence.

And now you can fully stop worrying about how other souls are completing their commission.

You can enjoy the release of such dire responsibility of other people's lives, 'cause you very truly cannot control it [sic].

You are only here to shine your light, because that is what you have agreed to do.

You cannot control the agreement of other soul's commission to see the light.

Some of them are not even meant to see it this time around. So you would really be in their way if you were trying to force them in a direction that they have no business going in at this time.

You are right.

You have fought battles in your other earthly lifetimes.

You have been outraged, and you have fought a great deal.

And good fights you have fought.

But now it is your time to rest—your time to enjoy, your time to be truly peaceful.

Some of what you will share, you will share through the writings we will send you. But much of what you will share is simply through your being in your everyday activities.

If you would like to understand more about the horrors or the difficult times, about the several past lives you have lived, investigate it freely and use the understanding.

But do not become sidetracked or absorbed in those details, because they are merely details.

Go now into your day and look forward to many magical events coming to you in the very near future.

Prepare yourself for a lot of writing and note taking. You may want to keep a notebook with you at all times now, because many coincidences and synchronicities will be happening, and it will be too hard to remember all of them to write down later.

Happy Easter. Happy springtime for all souls and all religions. This is truly a time for rejoicing throughout all the spheres of the universe. It is not a coincidence that Passover and Easter happen at about the same time of the year. Enjoy the renewal of this time.

CAROLE LYNNE IN HER OWN VOICE: Thank you. I am going to come out of the session now. I would very much like to have time today to type this out and add it to my notebook. Maybe even draw the visions of my homeland that I saw in my fantasy. Thank you.

Comments on the Session

So many things were said to me in this session: Be at peace. Stop being so busy. And remember that just because you are a teacher, you are not better than anyone else. You are a teacher because you need to be a teacher in this lifetime; those who are students need to be students.

I am overwhelmed as I reread the words that came through in this session. I was told that I do not have to worry about people rejecting me when I teach or reach out. What I have to offer is not helpful to those people in this lifetime. They are simply on another path!

This is wisdom for all of us, as so many of us worry and feel inadequate when people reject us. But when we look at rejection from the perspective of reincarnation, we can easily see that those who reject us need to reject us. If they were to accept our ideas, they might end up going in the opposite direction of where they need to go in this particular lifetime. Trying to persuade them to follow us is actually harmful to them. If we are all different, then it stands to reason that we all have different needs.

In this session, I was also given an image of Kapulpulpik as a place to refuel. My Guidance suggested that I have existed most of the time in another spiritual realm and that a life on earth is unusual for me. This was a very new and startling concept for me, but, even though I am a past-life agnostic, I was open to what has come through and to exploring the possibilities.

For example, consider the possibility that our spirits are alive and enter our physical bodies while we are still in our mothers' wombs, and that before our spirits enter our earthly bodies, they may have lived past lives on other planets or within other spiritual realms. It is possible that our spirits have even manifested as many different life-forms—life-forms that our scientists know nothing about.

Just for a moment, let's consider this question: is it possible that each one of us is born out of the energy of the entire universe? Most of us do not have a problem with the concept that energy never dies but is transformed. When a tree dies, its roots break down and become part of the soil, which one day gives birth to a new tree. In this case, the energy that once was the roots has now become energy of the soil, and ultimately within this soil energy, the energy of a new tree grows. While we readily accept the fact that energy is transformed within our planet and our universe, we do not often think about how energy is exchanged between universes and even other realms—realms that have not yet been discovered except within mystic revelations and visions.

This thought evokes several questions: What part have the energies of the entire universe played in who we are today?

In other words, are we made out of the energies of the entire universe?

Allow yourself to ponder this question: if it is true that we are made of the energies that travel throughout the universe, *and* if past lives do exist, then might it not be possible that as each individual's energy is transformed from one life to the next, some or most of the past lives of anyone living on the earth right now may have been lived on other planets and may have lived as other life-forms in another part of the universe? To be honest, I lie awake at night and ponder such questions. I ask myself, "Why do we assume that we have always been in the form we are in now? And why do we assume, with that *big* universe out there, that the energy that is you and the energy that is me right now has always been on this planet?"

Conclusions

While I remain an agnostic about past lives, I am open to the concept of reincarnation and waiting for an extraordinary personal experience that convinces me that the teachings of reincarnation are true. Because I have such great proof that we survive death, I am eager to have proof that we are born again and again. My Cambodian friend's story moved me closer to believing in reincarnation, and the messages I received about my past lives in the channeling sessions have also made an impression on me. Even though I don't yet have the definitive proof I need to believe in past lives, I do believe that the concepts of reincarnation are instructive to us all. First, they teach that we are here for a purpose and that each person has his or her own goals and needs within each lifetime. Second, they provoke fascinating questions and open new possibilities about the nature of the universe and our own existence.

Chapter 5

Why Riddles and Rhymes?

THROUGH THE AGES MEN AND WOMEN on the spiritual path have received teachings in the form of stories, riddles, and rhymes. But why does Spirit speak this way? Why doesn't the god of our understanding just tell us what to do in plain everyday language?

Whether you read the Bible or poetry by William Blake, you will find symbolic language. Whether you read poems by Robert Frost, Kahlil Gibran, Henry Wadsworth Longfellow, or Saint Augustine, you will find poetic images that speak to the soul. Poetic language does not always make sense to the logical mind, but it speaks to the soul in the same way the sudden appearance of a rainbow or an unbelievably beautiful sunset does.

Perhaps it is easier for us to experience the spiritual vibrations encoded in the words of a poem or story if those words do not immediately make sense. At that moment we have to stretch; we have to allow another part of our consciousness to take over in order to understand the words. Our rational "go-to-the-grocery-store" state of consciousness simply cannot make sense of the words, but our soul can.

In the early nineties, as I sat in my basement asking questions of a form of spiritual guidance, the answers often arrived in poetic language and stories. Here is an example, excerpted from a September 17, 1991, session.

CAROLE LYNNE STILL IN HER OWN VOICE: What is this passage that I am going through? I need your help. I ask for your guidance.

MY GUIDANCE: Sometimes the flower seems like it grows too tall

> When it is but a seed enveloping the whole of all its parts
> Penelope runs through the meadow
> The breezes in her hair
> Why, shooting through outer space, do you ride?
> A pinhead is a point for your attention

To be quite honest, as those words came out of my mouth and were recorded on my cassette player, I did not understand their meaning. Hours later, when I typed out the transcript of the session, I still did not understand. However, two sentences seemed to jump off the page of the transcript: "Why shooting through outer space do you ride? A pinhead is a point for your attention." Immediately, I had a vision of myself traveling all over the universe looking for answers when the answers were right in front of me—answers so small that they could fit on the head of a pin. The words stung me like a wasp and stopped me in my tracks.

Contemplate the image of the seed in this verse. When you think of a seed, do you not usually think of it as being inside a fruit such as an apple, a lemon, an orange, and an avocado? And when you think about the seed of a flower, do you not think of it growing into a flower? Yet in this short verse, the flower itself is a seed enveloping the whole of its parts. As I contemplate the image today, I see that the seed, or the beginning of something, is really the whole of it. Instead of the seed growing into an apple, a lemon, an orange, or an avocado, the fruit *is* the seed, which envelops the whole of its parts. I realize that this begins to sound like the riddle, "Which came first, the chicken or the egg?"

Here I was, feeling like a flower that was growing too tall, when I should have realized that I was really a seed enveloping the whole of myself—all of myself. And here was Penelope, with her feet on the ground, running through the meadow, while I, like a lost soul, was spinning through the universe looking for answers that were right in front of me if only I would *pay attention*. Aha! That was it. In order to understand myself—in order to understand my relationship to the universe—I had to plant my feet on the ground, like Penelope, and pay attention.

What a valuable message for all of us. Paying attention is one of the hardest things for us to do. Our minds are so busy; with thoughts flying around in every direction, it is hard for us to focus on the things that are important and that are often right in front of us. While we are in a conversation with one person, we focus on what we will be doing later. While our children are talking to us, we are thinking about the grocery list. We miss so much of our lives by failing to pay attention to what is going on in the moment.

Let us repeat these words over and over, and perhaps print them out and post them on the refrigerator or by the computer: "Why, shooting through outer space, do you ride? A pinhead is a point for your attention."

But what if Spirit had spoken to me in a more straightforward manner: "Hey Carole, plant your feet on the ground and stop searching for what is right in front of you." To be honest, I do not think I would have been moved at all, as those words would have sounded so common. They were words I have already heard a million times: "Carole do this. Carole do that." The fact that I could not easily understand the words forced me to go outside the box of my everyday thinking. I had to put my logical mind to the side so that my soul could get the message. My soul was affected not only by the words, but also by the energy that those words created within me.

How does the world of spirit speak to you? Are you ever drawn to a particular book, piece of music, or poem? Sometimes, when we are drawn in this way, we know that we are receiving a spiritual message. We know we are not just drawn to a certain song just because it is appealing. There is something about the way this song makes us feel; it evokes thoughts and emotions that have special meanings for us. Even messages on bumper stickers affect our emotions and thoughts this way and so deliver spiritual messages.

In October of 1991, another poetic piece came through that has mystified me for years. I have read this piece to groups, and I have set the words to music and sung them. The words force me to go outside of my everyday thoughts and into the experience of mystery.

As I began this session, the image of a camel first came into my mind. Then the mystical words began to flow.

> MY GUIDANCE: An old man rides on a camel lest he fall too soon
> Water springs where no man knows
> Love blooms where no man goes
> Sleep by the stars, and you shall see the meaning of eternity
> When a rose can bloom at night
> Then you have a second sight
> Going slowing it will bloom
> Into, into . . .
> Going slowly it will bloom
> Into, into . . .
>
> Cactus is a playful devil
> Jump around, and it will revel in the Mischievous of Owne
> And you will never find a home

Cactus is too dry, too stale
Cactus cannot tell the tale of wisdom
while the flower blooms with water seeping through its looms

Cradle love, and you shall see the wide expanse of mysteries
To love is always right in bloom
To find that other special room

As these words came through me, I knew for sure that I was connecting with an energy that was not part of the person I knew as Carole Lynne. I had been a songwriter for years, but these words were not in my writing style. I had never ever written anything like this.

As the words came, I was transported into a dimension of reality I had never experienced. I was suddenly in a desert—a place that I do not ordinarily think about. I was watching an old man ride a camel, because he could not walk through the desert. He would surely die if the camel did not transport him across the barren land. Next come images of water: "water springs where no man knows, love blooms where no man goes." Water was a substance both the camel and the man needed as they made their way across the desert. I was in a desert that had secrets; no man knows the mystery of the water in the desert. I was in a desert where love bloomed, but it bloomed in a place where no man goes. These words suggest that while love blooms in the desert, it blooms within another mystical dimension where a physical human being cannot enter. As these words penetrated my consciousness, I knew that I was being given a secret and mysterious knowledge.

The next words gave me the sense that I was flying through a mystery: "sleep by the stars, and you shall see the meaning of eternity." If I slept by the stars, I would have the answers and knowledge of all time. Do we not search for the answers that lie beyond this physical life? Do we not have questions about how we got here and where we are going, about the purpose of life and the existence of a Creator? Are these not the most important and intriguing questions that human beings ask?

As the words flowed, I received powerful energy for the spiritual journey ahead of me. Waves of mystical energy flowed through me. It felt like an initiation of some kind. What were these words, and where did they come from? Was their source a part of my subconscious that I had never experienced before? I sensed that the words came through my Greater Self, as this part of my consciousness is connected with Divine Consciousness. So I cannot give my subconscious credit for the experience. The part of me that must be reached in order to have the mystical experience seems far beyond both the conscious and the subconscious states of mind.

The Secrets Unfold with Riddles and Rhymes

We must be open to many levels of reality and ways of looking at reality. Theology, science, history, archeology, and psychology have all been trying to discover the truth about how life evolved and what life is. Science can prove many things about the evolution of our planet and the universe. There have been some good scientific experiments on spirit communication, and I hope that these experiments will continue. However, means of connecting with the world of the spirit cannot be enclosed in scientific theories and in the results of experiments. Spirit speaks to us in too many direct and personal ways that are not easy to test or evaluate. There are some spiritual experiences that go beyond our understanding, and these experiences cannot be fully tested. If you and I want to allow ourselves to merge with Divine Consciousness, we must allow ourselves to put logical thoughts to the side for the moment and listen to the language of the soul, which is very mystical and often poetic. While logic is a great tool, it is not the appropriate tool for every task imaginable. It is my impression that the spiritual secrets of the universe will not come to us through logical thinking. Riddles and rhymes take us into another level of consciousness, where we can perceive the ultimate truth.

Many life experiences help to take us out of our everyday thoughts and pave the way toward more spiritual realms. I can sit and weep watching the Disney movie *Pocahontas*. I can cry tears of joy watching *Pooh's Heffalump Movie*. These movies are for kids, but are we not all kids at heart? And if we become too sophisticated to enjoy a beautiful children's story, have we lost something? My daughter Jennifer is forty-two years old and a dedicated Disney fan: check out *www.brokehoedown.com*. She and our grandson have visited Disney parks around the world, and I am not sure if these trips are mostly for my grandson or my adult daughter. As a woman in my sixties, a trip to Walt Disney World takes me outside of myself and away from ordinary, every-day thoughts. Disney creates an environment where we can let our imaginations run free. Obviously Walt Disney World is not a spiritual site, but when I think about what it takes in order for most of us to let go of our structured thinking and our reasoning minds, the theme park is a great place to go to relax the mind. When I am at Walt Disney World, I get in touch with feelings of love and beauty. I feel empowered and feel that anything one can imagine is possible. It is odd, but Walt Disney's Tinkerbell may take me closer to the truth than many scientific theories can.

It is in letting go that we can receive from the world of the spirit. And that is why we receive many messages in riddles and rhymes: because these messages require us to venture outside our ordinary, everyday thoughts in order to understand them. Riddles and rhymes, stories and songs are great teachers.

Lessons for Everyone

~~~~~~~~~~

The following are two pieces received during channeling sessions. Embedded in these words are teachings for all of us. For the convenience of the reader, I have given each piece a title.

The Teacher

Before reading "The Teacher," a transcript of a channeling session from February 26, 1992, think about all the times in your life that you have tried to help someone or tried to control the actions of another person.

CAROLE LYNNE STILL IN HER OWN VOICE: I request My Guidance. I accept no other than the highest guidance for myself and for others. This morning I am thinking about a woman whom I occasionally do some work with, who is much younger than I, probably in her early to mid-twenties. She is very discouraged about the world. She is discouraged by the racism, the pollution, the corruption, and the lying that she sees that goes on by officials that keep facts from us about pollution. She is so discouraged that she does not want to bring children into this world. She has a discouraged and negative attitude about the world. I feel upset for her and wondered if she were here, what you would have to say to her or others who feel as she does.

(I count myself down into a light trance state.)

CAROLE LYNNE STILL IN HER OWN WORDS: I will speak the words that I hear My Guidance saying and soon the words will be simultaneously coming from My Guidance.

MY GUIDANCE: The red river of blood flows through the mountains and through the world, as it does through the veins of each individual human being.

There is darkness.

There is thunder.

There is lightning in the world of one who wishes to focus solely upon it.

Through the mud, through the mire, the diamond shows clear for all those who wish to see it.

The elephants march stoically across the desert, going in the direction that they know will bring them fulfillment.

The giraffes reach their necks high into the trees to find what they need.

Your friend is retreating and drawing her head within her body to a place where it cannot reach anything.

Each soul is confronted with many mirages and illusions and landscapes of reality.

Each must make their way and create the existence that is appealing to them in this lifetime.

Compassion, yes.

Sorrow, no.

Compassion for the feelings of despair.

Compassion for one who is not able to see the light around her.

Sorrow, no.

Because she creates her reality, as does each and every soul in the universe.

It is not your responsibility to show her the diamond.

She will see it, if it is her path and her wisdom.

Let the light of your diamond shine, and it will shine on her when you are with her.

And if she wishes to see it, she will.

Why Riddles and Rhymes?

And if it is not right for her to see it, she won't.

It is no concern of yours.

It is for you to mind your own business and create your own light.

Perhaps there is good reason for the darkness she sees now.

It is not for you to know.

Do not meddle with the universe or make assumptions beyond your own reality.

Compassion, yes.

Helpfulness, yes.

But the highest service is each soul's unique existence and journey.

To interrupt that is to murder.

Putting food into the mouths of hungry people, yes.

Putting clothes onto the backs of naked beings, yes, who are cold from the winter.

Putting thoughts into the minds of others, no.

So I have nothing to say to her this morning.

What I have to say is to you, and to tell you quite firmly, to mind your own business.

Such firmness you may not have heard from me before, but this is an extremely important issue.

What you do, you must do for yourself.

If helping others, if putting food in the mouths of others and clothes on the backs of others, is part of your soul's commission, then it is for you to do.

But ultimately you cannot do anything for anyone else.

You can be who you are, and those who need to receive who you are will flock to you.

And then it is not because of you.

It is because the light that is shining from you is the light that they are looking for at that time.

And you are not giving it to them.

You are simply letting it shine and those around you will do what they wish with it.

A good teacher is one who follows their soul's commission and allows others to view the process without really teaching them anything.

Without telling,

Without instructing,

Without pushing,

Without preaching,

But with simply being who you are and letting those who wish to model use the light that comes to them.

A great teacher is one who lives their soul's commission and therefore demonstrates the courage to do that.

A great teacher does not expect people to understand what they are doing,

To praise what they are doing,

To recognize what they are doing.

But they simply do what they are doing because it is what they are there to do.

Doing it for the sake of itself, and not for any of the rewards that may come.

A great teacher is one who has so much compassion for themselves,

And their own needs,

And their own dreams,

And their own soul's commission.

That they automatically will develop the compassion for other people's unique mission and will never try to force their mission on anyone else.

But instead will create an environment where students find it possible to find their own way, which in many cases will lead them away from the teacher to a different sphere of reality.

And that is as it should be.

The teacher should rejoice when the student cries, "No, I do not agree. I do not believe what you believe. *However, I believe what I believe.*"

And then the teacher has been a success because the student is believing, is finding their own reality, and that is what they are there for.

Go now into your day and see the world in the form of reality that you see it, and let others see it in theirs.

Thrive on the differences of perception.

That is all.

CAROLE LYNNE IN HER OWN VOICE: Thank you. That was very expansive.

We are all teachers of someone. We are parents, we are older siblings, we are grandparents, we are friends. We are school-teachers, tourist guides, writers, doctors, business managers, and construction managers. All of us are teachers of someone. What kind of teachers do we want to be? "The Teacher" helps us answer that question by describing the merits of modeling who we are. It tells us that to be the best teachers, we don't need to preach but simply need to have the courage to live out our own dreams. We don't need to teach as much as we need to let others learn from our actions. Looking back at the special teachers in your life, ask yourself why you found them to be such good teachers. Was it because they taught you? Or was it because they lived their lives in a way that helped you find your own way?

Honor the Beauty of Each Soul

Before reading this piece, reflect on the ways that you can help each person you know by honoring who they are. We can find beautiful ways to help others by being of service to them through our compassion and tolerance.

The question I asked My Guidance before channeling this next piece was "I feel myself flowing into a deeper level of commitment of service of other people. Would you like to speak to me about 'service' this morning?" The following is the answer I received on February 2, 1992.

> The moon serves the earth.
>> Life in many forms is available for service.
>> The moonside of your heart is available.
>> Open the petals one by one, and service shall flow from
> the center.
>> Sometimes service is waiting quietly and doing nothing.
>> Often the highest service is no action of any kind,
>> But simply the recognition of each soul's existence.
>> Honor the beauty of each soul, and the service will begin to flow
>> as a natural stream flows down a mountain.
>> Service can be found in all areas of life.
>> It does not need to be organized always.
>> Go today and experience the beauty of the universe.
>> That is all.

I was stunned by the idea that I had a "moonside" of my heart. What did that mean? While I still do not know, these words contained an energy that instantly ignited a connection between my heart, the moon, and the earth. I was suddenly bigger than my physical self; I was suddenly aware of how I existed in a different dimension. The words penetrated a deeper part of my consciousness. I am extremely grateful that the logical part of my personality, which wants a physical description and proof that a moonside of the heart exists, has been quieted and is not annoying me and trying to ruin my experience.

The answer to the question I asked when I began this session was so simple, so beautiful: "Honor the beauty of each soul, and the service will begin to flow as a natural stream flows down a mountain." Picture a natural stream flowing down the side of a mountain. The water is fresh and clear, and it generates a power as it flows—a natural power, a power that allows the "service to flow." This is a power that can be activated simply by honoring the beauty of each soul. My heart understood and accepted the fact that honoring each soul's beauty would be a real challenge for my personality. *"What?"* my personality cried. "I have to honor the beauty in everyone, and I can't always have my way? I have to stop competing with people and trying to be the best? I have to change? I am not so sure that I like this business of honoring the beauty of each soul!" Do you ever feel as I did? Do you want your own way? Do you want to always be the best?

Learning to honor the beauty of each soul is a lifelong challenge. Our personalities must work at it each day, because if we are truly honoring the beauty of each soul, we will be willing to step to the side so that others can shine. We will, at times, be willing to give up opportunities for ourselves so that others may move forward. Some will argue that there is so much opportunity to go around that we do not need to give up anything in order for others to succeed. While there is a truth to that idea, there is also a falsity. There are times when to serve others, we must stand back.

Our souls already know how to honor other souls. When our personalities try to drag us into energy that is overly competitive, intolerant, or greedy, each one of us can reach for the soul level, call to the spirit within—that part of each of us that is the Greater

Self, which is connected to Divine Consciousness. As we open up to the Greater Self, we can honor the beauty of each soul. And at that moment we will experience the peace that we have dreamed of. At that moment we will experience cosmic bliss, because we are, in that moment, connected to the Cosmic Divine.

When My Guidance says "Open the petals one by one, and service shall flow from the center," it is telling us that as we allow ourselves to open up to cosmic energy—love, truth, and compassion—we will find ourselves on a journey into the inner heart, the inner soul. And in this sacred place within, the compassion abounds and begins to flow. Compassion flows out from the center, to our loved ones and to the world. The journey into the inner heart is filled with images and poetic words. These experiences are our teachers.

Conclusions

~~~~~~~~

Divine knowledge is within and can be accessed as we open to the energies of cosmic reality. Everything that exists is part of the whole. Everything is within reach of our fingertips. Poetic language and stories open the doors for us. Let us be open to our visions and our stories, and retrieve the very old wisdom that each one of us has inside. I offer you the following words to contemplate which were received in a channeling session on December 25, 1992.

Seeing in All Directions
The rock
Seemingly solid
Is but a multitude of vibrations
The sky

Seemingly far away
Is at your fingertips
The ocean
Seemingly flowing
Is everywhere
In your body
In the air
The snow-topped mountain
Or the deep valley
Or the sky
Or the river
Are all within reach of your fingertips
The moon
The stars
Are in your heart
Reach out more easily
And all will come together without effort
Like the dancer who spins on one toe around and around
Seeing the world as she goes by staying in one place
You will now center yourself
And while staying in one place, centered within yourself
You will see all that is around you
As if you had eyes on every inch of your body
Seeing in all directions
Go now into your day with lightness and joy

Chapter 6

Many Births and Deaths within One Lifetime

~~~~~~~~~~~~~~~~~

Willows weep for the part of you that now dies.
It is a loss.
It is a giving up.
But robins sing and butterflies rejoice that your Higher Self is now
your vehicle for operation in the world.
Man lives in a shell that is but a vehicle for transportation of the soul.
It is nothing.
As it falls away, it is renewed.
Walk the road that comes to you.
Do not choose it.
Do not follow it.
Do not find it.
Simply walk it as it comes to you.
It will curve.
It will bend.
At times it will disappear from under your feet.
And you will fly instead of walk.
—WORDS OF MY GUIDANCE CHANNELED DECEMBER 19, 1992

IT IS HARD TO TALK about the separation I felt as I began to leave my old life and come into the path of spiritual unfoldment. My Guidance was telling me, "Walk the road that comes to you," and telling me that "at times it will disappear from under your feet." That was very hard for a woman in her forties, who had just been through the feminist revolution of the sixties and seventies, to hear. I had been learning to be a self-motivated woman all those years, to find my own road and walk my own path, and I believed that if I did so, I could have anything I wanted. Now some mystical energy, from who knows where, said nothing about my finding myself or my own path, but instead told me to walk the road that came to me. If I followed this advice, would I become utterly passive and ridiculous? At that time, I did not understand that it was only my personality that found this new idea absurd, but my soul was able to perceive the Truth. On the soul level, I knew that a road was coming to me that I had never dreamt of before. And it was that knowing within that prompted me to go downstairs into the basement most mornings for quite a few years, turn on my tape recorder, count myself down into what we would today call a state of trance or hypnotic state, and to ask questions and receive answers from an energy I would come to call My Guidance.

The Old Me Is Shed Like Leaves Falling from the Trees

I knew I was on a spiritual adventure and I was changing rapidly. I remember one lovely fall day, when the air smelled of autumn leaves, I took a walk in my neighborhood. As I walked, I had a vision of that which I had known as "myself" dying. But it was not death as we usually think of death. It was as if I were shedding an old skin, like a snake does, and underneath this old skin was a new person. I cried as I walked. I could feel my old, comfortable self, the self I had known all these years, being shed. It was extremely sad, because I knew I would never be the same again. I was now entering a realm where I would feel separated from many I loved and whom I did not expect to understand the "new" me. I was not frightened. I was very lonely.

I decided not to talk about what I was experiencing. I did not feel my family and friends were ready to hear me talk about voices from another realm that were guiding me. I thought they would accept me if I was writing fictional stories about spiritual experience. They would accept me if I went to a motivational self-improvement seminar and came back inspired to be a more powerful and successful person. But I did not expect them to understand what I was doing: receiving messages all by myself from a spiritual realm, sometimes in prose and sometimes in rhymes. I could not prove where the messages were coming from, and if I said I thought I was communicating with spiritual realms that we have not yet discovered, they would not believe me. I felt they would say that my imagination was running wild.

In 1987, when I started receiving messages, Neale Donald Walsch had not yet published his book *Conversations with God,* which came out in 1996. I was very alone with my experiences. Jane Roberts, who was claiming to channel a spirit named Seth, was just starting to publish books, but I was not really aware of them. I did speak often with and receive guidance from a well-known channel, Moriah Marston. She helped relieve my loneliness, and I learned a lot from her about how to take care of myself as I continued on with my channeling.

The more I channeled, the more I changed. I felt as if I were dying and being reborn, dying and being reborn. It was a spiritual cycle that I have come to know well. But when this cycle first began, I was overwhelmed and resistant to change.

On the ongoing mystical journey, spiritual light floods in and around me, and now, as then, I can sometimes hardly cope with the bright rays. Spiritual transformation is like walking into the bright sun without sunglasses. When the Divine light is too much for me, I put on the dark glasses of resistance in order to block from my internal vision the spiritual knowledge that is coming to me. As I take a step forward spiritually and feel overwhelmed, I then resist, and I take a step backward. Two steps forward, one step back, two steps forward, one step back—this is the best way for me to advance on the spiritual path. There are energetic changes within the spiritual seeker, as well as changes in one's personal and professional life. One cannot move too quickly.

Energetic and Personal Changes

As the early messages came through, I was told "the light that is your voice is still cloudy, and some of the colors cannot shine as yet." When I began to link with the energy that I call My Guidance, powerful vibrations entered my body. But I was simply not a good vessel to contain or hold this powerful energy. I felt dizzy, nauseous, and extremely sleepy!

As the messages came, my view of the world changed. I can appreciate what it must have felt like for people who thought that the world was flat to learn that it was round. I used to live in a world that revolved around the sun and was part of a universe that included other planets, which I had been told did not show any signs of life. My life was centered on being married, raising kids, working as a musician, and surviving the crazy times in the seventies and eighties. Now I became aware that my soul may have existed or traveled not only to other planets, but also within realms and dimensions that we cannot see with any of our current scientific instruments. I was disoriented, to say the least!

I used to see myself as a simple human being. I would live my life, die, and who knows what would happen after death. I called myself an "afterlife agnostic." Now I began to see myself as a multidimensional being with a physical body and, more important, a spirit that would survive when my physical body was of no use to it any longer. I learned that my spirit travels in many dimensions that my body cannot visit and my conscious mind cannot access. With all these changes, energetic and personal, it is no wonder that I had to take two steps forward and one step backward. I needed, and still need, to resist sometimes, pretend to myself that I am a simple person and take a break from being me.

"What Do You Do?"

Before I knew I was a channel for Spirit and a psychic medium, when someone on an airplane would ask me, "What do you do?" I would say that I was a coach for public speakers and performers. This answer often led to me listening to tales of people's experiences with music. Then people would ask my advice on what kind of guitar strings to buy, when children should start music lessons, and how to hire the right band for a wedding. Or they would ask me if everyone has stage fright before giving a business presentation.

Now when someone asks, "What do you do?" and I answer "I am a psychic medium," what follows is a silence so loud it almost hurts your ears. Then the silence is followed by "Oh, how interesting" and that is the end of the conversation, or by "Wow, do you see any spirits around me right now?" or "Can you tell what I am thinking?" These days I often tell people that I am a retired singing teacher, as I cannot always cope with conversations with strangers about my spiritual life.

As many of you on the spiritual path know all too well, the path leads to many social and personal changes. Once you have opened yourself to the Divine, life on earth is never the same. It is more wondrous, but there are many ups and downs. As we put on our spiritual roller skates, we are going to skin our knees.

Spirit Speaks to Me to Ease My Death and Rebirth

The early messages that flowed through me were intoxicating. As I felt my old self dying, Spirit would speak to me, sending me words that urged me to go forward in my spiritual quest. The following words from Spirit, which I received during a channeling session on December 30, 1992, have continued to help ease the pain as I go through spiritual cycles of death and rebirth.

> Turquoise waves of color so bright I am blinded by the beauty of the waves of color on my eyelids.
> Swelling rivers of emotion are gliding across the seas of my mind.
> On occasions, I am dancing with the wind in the most impossible circles and triangles that envelope us as we swoon and mix with the elements of the cosmos.
>
> No, she cried, it cannot be that this world really exists in such splendor and beauty as I can see at this moment in time and space, which a moment of golden dew can erase.
>
> Come, said the brook, and I will take you to a land where the oranges grow on apple trees and everything is not as you would expect it to be.

Where camels drink of nectars that they never knew existed before, and maidens are maidens no longer but goddesses against the wind with perfumed longings.

Stroll with me into a land where never is never and imagination is the beauty so splendid that you cannot imagine it—ha ha!

Grapes are not grapes but succulent morsels to be guided into places where grapes have never been, and you will mingle with textures and silences and lights and darknesses that you have never seen or heard or witnessed on the earth.

What is a man but a fragment of time in space like a little grape on a vine?

Why do you worry so about what will happen to you?

You are not even there in the total sense of the world.

You are but a grape on the vine, waiting to ripen and blend into eternity, the sweet wine of existence on another plane.

Come, Carole, do not be afraid of the path that we take you down.

It is not a path at all.

It is right there in front of you to be touched by our energy at any moment you desire.

You do not have to go far away into the cosmos, but instead you can stay right where you are and feel the sweetness of the nectar that we sing of.

The sweet sounds that you heard in your mind are the sounds of angels who are singing for you and those around you that care to listen.

Do not turn them away or shut them up because someone else does not believe. After all, what do they believe in but fragments that they have imagined and created into reality?

Many Births and Deaths within One Lifetime

You have as much right as they do to create the reality that gives you pleasure and sends you to the god of your heart.

Do not be trapped into realities that you do not wish to create.

Some realities may be fine for others but not for you.

You are the master of your own reality.

Come down the path of your spiritual soul, and you will see such wonders that you have never seen or heard or imagined.

It will be a gift of such proportions.

It will be enormous in content and desire and security.

You hesitated when I said "security."

Yes, security is what I mean. There is no security in the hatred and animal instincts of the killers on the earth.

You do not wish to be part of that energy.

So leave that energy and come to the land of love and peace and security with the values and proportions of the fragments that present themselves to you now.

Do not be afraid.

Your sense of humor will carry you through the times when it is all too unbelievable to be real.

But in time you will come to know that we are real and that we have been with you for a long time.

You have been with us for a long time, and so we are really old friends.

It is only the earth, Carole, who holds you back now. It is time for you to remember your home, and you will feel safe and happier on the earth.

Ring the bells of silence, and you will hear the most incredible music that you have ever not heard.

It is not the hearing of the earth. It is the hearing of angels of such sweet sounds that they will remain with you throughout the day.

Sing with the angels, and they will sing with you.

As I read these words today, I remember how invited I felt—invited to a whole new range of experiences that would take me into realms I had never experienced. The words that came through my mind that day wanted to turn my image of the world upside down: I was invited to imagine that "oranges grow on apple trees," and I was told that everything would not be as I expected it to be. Some of the language was sensual and almost sexy in nature: "Grapes are not grapes but succulent morsels to be guided into places where grapes have never been, and you will mingle with textures and silences and lights and darknesses that you have never seen or heard or witnessed on the earth."

I was so happy to hear the words "[t]he sweet sounds that you heard in your mind are the sounds of angels who are singing for you and those around you that care to listen." I had been hearing, and I continue to hear, incredible music that I know other ears do not. I hear this music with what I call my "spiritual ears." I realize some people may label my experience as an auditory hallucination, but my soul knows that I am hearing music from other realms.

At first this image of "bells of silence" did not make any sense to me. But as I thought about it and let those words flow through my inner self instead of my intellectual mind, I realized that silence had its own incredible sound and that every moment of silence is as unique as every moment of sound. Within silence is music, and within silence is Truth. We commonly think of sound as something that we hear with our ears. But the real truth may be that the music exists whether we hear it with our physical ears or not. Some of us are fortunate enough to hear the music with our spiritual ears.

After receiving words such as these, I was excited and motivated to continue my search. But what was I searching for? What was so appealing? What called to me so strongly? There was and is a pull, a yearning that, like an irresistible magnet, pulls some of us toward the Divine light. Once one has experienced this light, there is no turning back. And as we move forward we change; it is difficult to give up the old self, however appealing the Divine may make things look.

Spirit Speaks about My Living Death

On March 24, 1993, I received the following words from My Guidance:

> You are the rose at full bloom now.
> The old you is dying a very painful death.
> The old you is kicking and screaming
> and causing anxiety attacks.
> As you try to hold on to the values that were once realistic for you, the old ways of doing things do not service.
> You must let go of the parts that are not appropriate for you anymore. It is okay.

Changing was very scary. I asked My Guidance, "How do I take care of my ego as I go through this change? Am I in the world just to be of service to people? What are the parts to hold on to for myself? How can I be of true service to others without becoming a doormat?"

I did not want to be a doormat. I thought it would be terrible to give up who I had become and instead become a doormat for people to step on.

But My Guidance obviously did not have the same concept of a doormat:

> Doormats are entrances to a whole new world.
>
> A doormat can be seen in several different ways.
>
> One may step upon your shoulders in order to go through an entrance into a new place.
>
> A doormat is not such a terrible place to be.

I had never thought of a doormat this way. But when you think about a doormat, where is it placed? Near a door, and a door is an entrance.

Well, if a doormat could be something other than what I thought it was, then what about a table, a person, a country, the world, the cosmos, or my relationships? I was beginning to understand that while in many ways my life would look the same, it would no longer be the same. I was transforming energetically, and I could now begin to see myself and the world around me in many different ways.

With my change in the concept of a doormat, I was willing to become a doormat, or, if you like, an entrance, because other people would be stepping on my shoulders to enter a whole new world. What a concept! The thought of it all made me feel both dizzy and excited.

On that same day, Spirit spoke to me about "the lily":

> The lily winding down the stream goes slowly at times because the currents, which are moving back and forth and sideways, although they may be moving at a very rapid rate, the combination of currents produce slow movement for the lily.
>
> And yet the lily does not mind the slow movement because she will see each flower and each tree and each twig and each squirrel and each bird that she passes as she continues down the river.

Be like the lily.

Find the earth.

Find the natural substances.

And do not allow your life to become encased in a tin-can environment.

When I think of a lily floating in the water, I think of gentle movement, but I do not think about lilies that move slowly down the river. Of course, if a lily broke loose from the lily pad, it would move with the currents of the waters. And as this image comes to my mind, I see myself as a lily that is breaking loose and flowing down the river. The currents of the river are crossing each other in a manner that sometimes has me floating gently in the same place, and then, as the currents change, I float down the river. Spirit is telling me that I must move slowly and gracefully, observing whatever happens along the way, allowing the currents to either move me along or keep me in the same position for a while.

At the time of this session, I was in a state of anxiety about the self I saw fading away. I found the words about the lily to be comforting, stabilizing, and extremely calming. Spiritual changes are energetic changes; when one is not used to making energetic changes, they can be disorienting. The energetic rug was being pulled out from beneath my feet, and I was not sure who I was going to be as the old energy was being replaced by the new. I was a snake shedding old skin to reveal new skin that was tender and vulnerable. And I am new and vulnerable every time I go through another transition and shed yet another skin. I am the caterpillar who has been crawling along the ground, then has rested, enclosed in a cocoon, and finally emerged as a butterfly. This cycle has been repeated over and over for me on the spiritual path.

Cycles of Rebirth: From Old Me to New Me

Words from My Guidance:

> Plums ripen just as they are supposed to,
> and the sweet smell fills the air.
> Allow yourself the ripeness of your journey.
> Allow yourself the pungent odor, even though at times you may
> fear that you are rotting.
> You are not rotting.
> You are simply falling away into a greater existence.
> And that which you are shedding will simply go back into the
> Universal Energy and be used by someone else.
> It never belonged to you anyway.
> It was only a fantasy, a fiction, used for a certain time.
> You can call on your remembrance of it occasionally and play
> with it, if you like.
> But the real core of your soul will be coming through now,
> and that is how you will be living.
> It is okay.

It is not new for me to believe that when I die, my spirit will live on. But is it new for me to consider that when I feel a part of me "dying" and being "reborn" within the span of my earthly life, that old part of me will simply go back into the Universal Energy and be used by someone else. If you stop to think about the ramifications of that thought, it is astounding. All that I am and all that I experience is borrowed clothing that I wear for a while and then give back to a "central energetic clothing station," where someone else can pick them up and wear them as long as they are needed. It means that all that I think I am is really just a projection of what

I am learning at the moment, and when I no longer need to see myself in this projected view, it simply vanishes and is replaced by an updated version.

It is one thing to say, "Oh, I have changed, and I am not like I used to be." We all say that. It is quite another thing to realize that our old self is simply a projected energy that is wrapped around our spirit until it is no longer needed. You and I are not as permanent as we think we are, even when we are living in a physical body on this earth. On the spiritual path, we experience many deaths and births within one lifetime.

If you are experiencing the cycles of death and rebirth within this lifetime, do not be alone. Find others to share your thoughts with. Join a spiritual group whose ideas are similar to yours. If you are in extreme pain, find a therapist with a spiritual orientation and ask for the help you need. Spiritual progress is not always easy.

Today I am joyful. I have been through the cycles of spiritual change often enough now to be able to withstand them without a lot of emotional pain. Spiritual change is like riding a bicycle. After awhile, you get used to it and enjoy the ride.

PART TWO

The Higher Cosmic Realms

Chapter 7

A Little Girl Makes a Deal with God

~~~~~~

WHEN I WAS A LITTLE GIRL, growing up and going to a Congregational church with my grandmother and later a Presbyterian church with my sister, I saw God as a being who sat in heaven and spoke to me. In other words, my view of God was personified. I was also taught that Jesus Christ was the Son of God and that he died for our sins, and that when Adam and Eve disobeyed God's laws in the Garden of Eden, from that point on all children would be born in sin. It was only through the salvation of Jesus Christ that I could be saved and go to heaven when I died. I understood clearly that those who were not Christians would not go to heaven, but to a terrible place called hell.

While, as a child, I could feel the love of God and Jesus in my heart, I had a bit of a problem with the teaching that those who were not Christians would go to hell at the end of their human lives. My father was Jewish, as were my grandparents, aunts, uncles, and cousins on my father's side. I found it hard to believe that my mother's Christian side of the family had a chance to go to heaven, but my father's family did not. This was not a problem that I felt comfortable discussing with either of my parents, so

I took this problem to God. After all, he should know, as these were supposedly his rules.

God and I got along just fine, and I felt protected and loved. I knelt by my bed often and talked to God about all that went on. The beauty of this relationship sustained me through many family challenges, and I treasured my time with God. However, I did not resolve my confusion about heaven and hell. I received no answers or explanations and continued to wonder how God, whose presence I felt, could ever do anything but help people when they died—no matter who they were.

When it came time for my Christian confirmation, I stood before the pastor of our church and the congregation to repeat my vows. As I did so, I had my fingers crossed behind my back. As I repeated the vows out loud, I had my own inner and silent conversation with God. I said, "While I am repeating these vows, I need you to know that I do not believe all that I am saying. I believe in you, God, but I do not believe in all that I have been taught. I feel that somehow those around me do not have the real story about who you are. I am committing myself to you, God, as I am being confirmed today, but I am not confirming to you or to myself that I believe all of the words I am repeating and ways of thinking about you that I have been taught."

Looking back on this early childhood spiritual experience, I am aware of how important it was for me, a child of about thirteen, to be truthful to God. I didn't mind repeating these vows, but I did not want to lie to God, because I knew that it was God who was supreme and not the church. I was not angry at the church. I just felt that the leaders of the Presbyterian churches were very well-meaning people who had not gotten it right as far as God and heaven were concerned. I kept these views to myself for a very long time.

A Deal Is Made

One day, on a beautiful spring morning in church, I made an important deal with God. While sitting on the choir bench waiting to sing with the choir, I saw a sphere of light flood the church— light that I felt others did not see and that was directed right at me. It was as if I left my physical body and my spirit merged with that sphere of light for a conversation with God. I was told that I was being called to help others during my life on earth. As a young teenage musician and actress, I protested and told God that I wanted to be on the stage. I wanted to go into show business. God listened in the calm manner that I had come to expect and then told me, "OK, Carole, for the first half of your adult life you will be a performer and do all the things you want to do. Then in the second half of your adult life you will work for me." That sounded extremely reasonable, and so after thinking about it for a few minutes, I agreed, and a spiritual deal was made.

A Middle-Aged Woman Keeps the Bargain

God kept his part of the deal and paved the way for my work as a musician during my twenties, thirties, and forties. I had a great time working as a singer/dancer on TV shows produced in Manhattan, being part of Equity summer stock companies, working as a singer on TV and radio commercials, and working as a singer/guitarist in many clubs in New York, California, and Massachusetts. I also had a busy practice coaching singers and public speakers.

It was during my forties and early fifties that I began to have clear visions of Spirit, started channeling, and joined a Spiritualist church. My ability to see those who have passed over came on very quickly, and before I knew it, I was working on Spiritualist platforms, doing demonstrations of spirit communication. My professional life began to change; I needed to stop performing in concerts and stop coaching musicians and public speakers in order to have time to do readings and demonstrations. I kept my bargain with God.

As I look back, I wonder if I would have had visions of Spirit earlier in my life if I had not made that bargain with God. As a child, I had agreed that while I was willing to work for God in whatever way God had in mind, I wanted to be a performer first. Perhaps God actually kept visions of spirits from me until I had the opportunity to work as a musician and was ready to take on the responsibility of being a psychic medium. As I realized I was a psychic medium, I knew it was going to be a huge responsibility—a spiritual path, quite frankly—that I would not have been mature enough to cope with when I was younger.

An Older Woman Evolves and Sees God in a Different Light

I am now in my sixties. I still have a deep love of God, but I do not see the personified God I saw at age thirteen. He is not an old man sitting up in heaven directing me. In fact, the God of my understanding is not a he or a she and has no personality as we as human beings think of personality. I see God as Cosmic Energy—Spiritual Light. God is Divine Consciousness far beyond my human comprehension. I do not have adequate understanding or words to accurately describe God. I still have a love of Jesus, but I see Jesus in a different context than I did as a child. For me, Jesus remains in my heart, but as one of the greatest spiritual teachers, healers, and mediums who ever lived. I believe the spirit of Jesus still guides us. And I still believe Jesus is a son of God, but he is a son of God as we are all sons and daughters of God. I have come to value not only Jesus, but also many other great spiritual teachers, such as Buddha and Gandhi.

If God is beyond human comprehension and we have no adequate words to describe God, then how can we, as human beings, comprehend God? This question is extremely important, because as we come to understand that God is beyond our comprehension, we can begin to understand why God—or, as many of us say, Spirit—needs to speak to us in ways that we can comprehend: through spiritual dreams, revelations, synchronicities, and mystical experiences. As God speaks, Divine Consciousness flows through the mind of each individual soul. But because our mental perceptions differ based on our age, nationality, cultural upbringing, and possibly past-life tendencies, we do not each receive the messages from Divine Consciousness in the same way. Even though the Divine Consciousness is always the same, our perceptions of it differ. And that is as it should be.

Intuitive Yoga

Even though in my childhood view God was personified, I realize that at an early age I experienced God not just as a being, but as Divine energy. I remember being a young teenager, kneeling at my bedside for an hour, feeling the presence. I could feel the energy swirl around my physical body and become part of me. I felt the need to move into different physical positions as I prayed. Later on in life, I would recognize some of the positions that I moved into as the postures of yoga. As a child, I knew that I felt better physically when I allowed the power of the energy to move me into various postures. Intuitively, I was discovering yoga on my own. I believe the Spirit of God was healing me in those early days.

Even though my perception of God has been through many changes, I still feel the same spiritual presence around me that I had felt as a little girl.

An Eternal Investigation

~~~~~~~~~~~~~~~~

I have kept my bargain with God. I work as a psychic medium and spiritual teacher. I also volunteer many hours of my week to my Spiritualist church activities. But I have many questions about what I experience as I communicate with the world of spirit. How am I, as a psychic medium, able to communicate with the spirits of people who have passed into eternal life? How am I, as a channel, able to bring through inspirational stories and poems that I could never write in an everyday state of consciousness?

As a mature adult, I have also wanted to understand more about the spiritual presence that had always been with me. What is this Spirit? How do I connect with Spirit? Where is the world of spirit? What is the spiritual presence that I channel that I name "My Guidance"?

In 2004 I was working as a psychic medium, but still hiding the fact that I was a channel. That was about to change.

Chapter 8

The Sitting Project

About the Project

IN 2004, THE TAPES AND TRANSCRIPTIONS of my early channeling sessions were still hidden away. The notes on the man-in-the-mountain dream and the vision of Saint Genevieve were in a notebook stuffed way back in a drawer. But I sensed my spiritual path might be taking a turn that would allow me to share my channeled work, as well as my observations and thoughts about that work.

Now I found that when I channeled, I was going into a deeper altered state of consciousness than I had in the early years. I suspected that I was going into a trance state. I laughed about the television commercials that said "do not try this at home" and realized that was exactly what I was doing: channeling at home all by myself when perhaps it was no longer a safe way for me to work. By this time, my association with the Spiritualist community had taught me the terms *trance medium* and *sitter*—terms I had not known when I started channeling in 1987. I suspected that the channeling I was doing was trance mediumship and that it was time to invite sitters to work with me. The job of the sitter is to observe the medium in trance and to interact with the spirit if a spirit speaks through the medium. The sitter also protects the medium from staying in trance too long or from any noises or interruptions that can be dangerous to the entranced medium's well-being.

I knew I had to find sitters whom I could trust completely. Mediums do not know what they are going to say in a trance session, and I would not be able to work effectively if I had sitters who were gossips. I also needed people who could devote the time needed to our work over a period of many years. In short, I had to find two incredibly honest people who had lifestyles that would allow them to make a solid commitment to our work. Not easy people to find!

I had, for the past few years, been facilitating a spiritual circle at my home that we called the Monday Night Circle. We began on September 10, 2001, the night before our whole world changed on September 11. After about three years, the work of the Monday Night Circle was beginning to come to a close, as various members became too busy to regularly attend. (In spiritual circle work, the energy must be consistent, which means having the same people present at every session.) During the years of the Monday Night Circle, I got to know Ron Monroe and Bob Blake, and I hoped that they would join me in my channeling sessions.

I was extremely nervous about inviting sitters to join me, even though my British friends had been urging me to do so. I found myself telling them, "In America I am going to have a very hard time finding anyone who will be able to put their own ambitions aside and sit regularly for me. Why should they? Americans are too egocentric, and they will not want to spend a whole evening devoting themselves to my work as a trance medium." But I was wrong. Not only did Ron Monroe and Bob Blake accept my invitation to be sitters, but both of them also seemed to understand that even though

I would be the person the spirits would be speaking through, our work together was for all three of us. We would all learn a great deal from the messages that came through. Ultimately, we were working together in the hopes of receiving spiritual knowledge that we could share with larger groups of people.

Meet Ron Monroe and Bob Blake

I invited Ron because he is a medium, and I invited Bob because he is not a medium. Ron Monroe has been psychic and mediumistic all his life. He has been certified in healing and mediumship by the American Federation of Spiritualist Churches and is now enrolled in the federation's ministry course. Ron is also a respected medical professional. A very smart man in whatever he does, he is able to look at facts in a realistic manner and at the same time turn his psychic vision to outer space and spiritual realms.

In his early childhood, Ron lived in a house that saw spirit activity, which his family was able to hear and witness. At that time, he didn't understand the world of spirit. He also didn't understand his own psychic-mediumistic nature and was frightened by the thought of it. He later learned that his great-grandmother and his grandfather had many spiritual experiences.

As a member of the Pentecostal church, he was exposed to the realities of spiritual healing and of various gifts of the spirit. He contemplated becoming a Pentecostal minister, but then decided to postpone any spiritual or religious studies. Eventually, he found his way to a Spiritualist church through a coworker, whose mother was a Spiritualist minister. I met Ron when, after finding my bio on *www.bestpsychicmediums.com*, he called me for an appointment, and I did a mediumistic reading for him. He began to attend my mediumship classes and joined the Plymouth Spiritualist Church. Since I have known Ron, he has been devoted to his work in the religion of Spiritualism.

Because he is a medium and can see clairvoyantly, I knew that Ron would be able to see what was happening to me on a spiritual and energetic level. He would be able to see the energy field around me and know if a spirit was trying to communicate through me.

Bob Blake, on the other hand, is not a medium, so he serves as an anchor for the whole group. For instance, while Ron and I may sometimes clairvoyantly see sparks of light floating around the room, Bob will not see them. Ron and I see the sparks subjectively, within our minds. If Bob were to also see the sparks, then we would know that the sparks were manifesting in a material way that can be seen by the physical eye, not just the spiritual eye. Ron and I are also very excitable and creative, and we need someone like Bob around to challenge us and say, "Well, I am not sure about that vision because I do not see it."

Bob is a no-nonsense, logical-thinking retiree, who helps his wife with their beautiful garden and travels to make use of their many timeshare weeks. An English major, he worked for many years in the alumni-relations department of M.I.T.; since retiring he continues to do the volunteer work he has done for many years for his alma mater, Dartmouth College. Although he grew up in a Congregational family, he was not particularly religious. In later life, when looking for comfort after his father died, a visit to a Spiritualist church helped him. He continued his spiritual journey by joining the Monday Night Circle and becoming a sitter in our channeling sessions.

From my perspective, Bob is not the typical person I would expect to see around spiritual circles, and yet he has an extremely psychic and mystical side, although he does not seem to realize it.

When the Monday Night Circle met, Bob sat to my right. There were dozens of times I would be thinking about something I might like to say and then Bob would say it. It was as if he were picking up on my thoughts. Bob also expresses himself very poetically at times, yet he can turn around and ask very challenging, intellectually based questions. Bob may ultimately discover that he has mediumistic abilities and can see the same clairvoyant images that Ron and I see. If that happens, then we will have three mediums in our group and have to find a new non-mediumistic person to serve as our anchor.

The Sitting Project Is Launched

We decided to call our work with the world of spirit "the Sitting Project," and we launched it in December 2004. The three of us did not know what would happen as I sat in an altered state of consciousness. In my early days of solo channeling, many poems and stories came through, along with guidance for me. Would there be poems and stories as there had been in the past? Would there now be guidance for all of us?

During our first few meetings as a group, our experience matched what other trance mediums experienced: the spirits of different people who have passed on spoke through me and brought messages to Ron and Bob. In some cases, spirits who came through had just passed over and needed our prayers to help them into the eternal life. During one session, a spirit who identified himself as Aron said that he had left a wife and two children living in Africa. We spent the session doing what many mediums call rescue work. As I allowed the spirit of Aron to speak through me, Ron and Bob encouraged Aron to move toward the light and make his transition into the eternal world.

With the launching of the Sitting Project, *My* Guidance was no longer specifically *mine*, as there were now three of us receiving advice. Bob received advice on how to proceed in some of his current projects, Ron was told that he needed to slow down and simplify his life, and I was told that I needed to trust the world of spirit more as I moved on in my channeling work.

All three of us needed the energy that I called My Guidance to prove its authenticity. We needed to have some information come through that I, Carole Lynne, had no previous knowledge of. For example, in the first year of the Sitting Project, Bob asked My Guidance where he could find some jewelry he had lost, and he was given a specific description of where it was. He then found the jewelry where My Guidance had said it would be. My Guidance told Ron things about his mother that neither Bob nor I knew anything about. In addition, My Guidance told him that his parents were going to have problems with water in their house. At the time, he knew nothing about any such problems, but within a couple months, his parents had to replace some water pipes. I had not known where Bob's lost jewelry was, and I had not known what was going on with Ron's parents and their house. The evidence that came through made us all comfortable that I was receiving communication from a source other than my own conscious mind.

What we did not yet understand was the complex nature of the energy I was channeling and how I, as a channel, brought through the messages.

From the beginning, I had realized that the energy I was channeling was not like the spirit guides I'd heard so many of my friends speak about. I had heard many people talk about their guides—"I am channeling a nun in a blue habit" or "I am channeling a Native American wearing a long headdress"—but I could not relate to their stories. I had the sense that I was channeling a presence that had never lived on the planet earth.

Years before the Sitting Project began, I had attended a seminar on trance. The teacher knew nothing about my experiences with My Guidance. While in the trance state, he told each one of us in the room about our spirit guides. Before he came to me, he spoke to approximately five other students. In each case, he described the student's guide as the spirit of someone who had lived on earth. When it was my turn, he stopped and paused for quite some time. Then he told me that he could see a white energy around me. He said that energy had never lived on the earth plane and was not like the other spirit guides he had just described to other students in the class. For me, this reading confirmed what I had suspected for years but had been afraid to talk about. Even though I personified the energy that was my guide, giving it the name *My Guidance* and speaking to it as if to another human being, My Guidance was not the spirit of a human being and had never been a living being on the earth.

In 2005, when we had been sitting together for about a year, the work in the Sitting Project began to change. Ron, Bob, and I learned, over a series of sessions, about the complex, universal, and cosmic aspects of what I had been calling My Guidance.

The Sitting Project Transcripts

Note: Some of the following transcripts have been shared in their entirety, and others have been partially shared. I have tried to present these channeling sessions as they happened. It is important for the reader to remember these are transcripts of words that were originally spoken.

The words of the sitters and the words I say when I am speaking in my own voice have occasionally been edited for clarification. We have taken out the usual "ums" and "ahs" and remarks that are not necessary for understanding what the sitter or I was trying to ask or explain. Extremely minimal edits have been made to the words I received as the channel from Spirit—even when these words may not immediately make sense to us or when the words are not grammatically perfect. We have filled in missed words that could not be heard on the tape only if, based on the context of what was being said, it is completely clear what these words must have been. There are several places where we have never been able to understand the missed words on the recordings. In those cases, we've noted that there are missed words.

Comments in parentheses are comments made for the reader's clarification and are not part of the original transcript.

The transcript of a session may be followed by post-session comments made by everyone who attended; these comments include the reactions we had and the lessons we learned and were often as informative as the session itself. At times I have presented the actual dialogue that we had after a session, and in other cases I give an account of what we spoke about.

My individual comments about what I learned from each session follow the post-session comments from the group.

December 15, 2005: A Universal Realm

"[A]ll of the universe is connected in a way
that no one even has any inkling of yet."

In attendance:
Channel: Carole Lynne
Sitter: Ron Monroe
Sitter: Bob Blake

My Guidance, which had been giving me advice for years and to the sitters during the first year of the Sitting Project, unexpectedly went cosmic on us. Suddenly, we found ourselves in front of a door leading into a much vaster world of spirit—a door none of us had entered before. Imagine that My Guidance is an announcer broadcasting from a tiny local station, and all of a sudden he is broadcasting from a realm in the cosmos. We went from hearing everyday advice to receiving messages about the nature of the energy that spoke through me and about spheres of truth encoded in light and interplanetary functions. The following is a partial transcript of the December 15, 2005, session.

As this session began, Ron counted slowly from ten to one, as I went into a deeper state of relaxation. I was able to ask a question in my own voice before going into a deeper state of consciousness, where I would only feel my lips and the rest of my mouth. Next I heard words in my mind that seemed to come from another realm. I repeated what I heard, and within a minute, there would be no lag time between what I heard and what I was saying. At this point, I felt that the words from another source were flowing through me.

> CAROLE SPEAKING STILL IN HER OWN VOICE: I need to ask you a question first. How am I going to get used to channeling with other people?

(Pause as I go into a deeper state to receive the answer)

> MY GUIDANCE: It will be the greatest lesson you have ever learned in your life. There is a way you have always separated yourself from people, not wanting to show certain vulnerabilities and wanting to feel safe. As you learn to be vulnerable and, in a sense, expose yourself in this way, you will find a universal love of people that goes far beyond what you have ever experienced. While this may be very scary, it is very far reaching, not only to your life on earth, but to your work after you leave this life. You resisted the idea of reincarnation, but now you are beginning to see that it is true. You did

choose to come here to do this work, and when this lifetime is over you will continue it. What John said the other night when you spoke with him about the writing, he said you were not looking for this; it came to you at a very young age. You have complete conviction, and you must go forward. This comes from a man who really does not believe in all this, but senses the truth in the communication.

Communication is like a long line of energy that flows from one to the other; it is like a wire, never ending, never broken, spiraling and twirling throughout eternity. Messages come from far, far in the universe; they do not take years to get here, like they say in NASA talk. These messages are instant, and all of the universe is connected in a way that no one even has any inkling of yet. Quantum physics is nothing compared to the understanding of energy that flows from planet to planet: universal energy. When this is discovered, human beings will finally understand what God is: that it is the energy of the universe, and that these spheres of light are the truths. Each night, when you go to sleep, you visit these places, as do many others who live on earth.

We feel the calmness in your vibration, Carole, as we talk about this. That is where your true interest is. When we talk about interplanetary functions, your energy calms. That is where you come from. So we have given a bit to think about.

(Ron and Bob are stunned by the change in the energy and by the messages that come through. Bob comments on the difference in the interaction. Ron observes colors around me that he had not seen before.)

BOB: I am interested and intrigued by this new way of interacting. It is a much more formal interactive process, and I guess I am at somewhat of a loss as to what questions to ask. I would appreciate whatever guidance you think appropriate.

The Sitting Project

RON: I am seeing different colors as you speak through Carole. Is this a result of the lighting in here or am I seeing different colors?

MY GUIDANCE: It has nothing to do with the lighting. It is the vibrations of healing we are bringing forward. You are seeing blues, and you are also seeing sort of pink, fuchsia, aren't you?

RON: Yes I am.

Comments

Imagine what it must have felt like to me to be told that I am more comfortable with interplanetary functions, because that is where I come from. I had a tough time because I was always the first one to think that people who said they channeled beings from other planets, or had originally come from another planet, were nuts. Now here I was channeling a voice that was telling me I was more comfortable in interplanetary functions. My rational mind was not happy at all, but my inner self knew that there was something very true about what had come through in this message.

Today, as I read the transcript, I am intrigued by the words "these spheres of light are the truths." Over and over, the words and images that have come to me give me a sense that Divine Consciousness is energy as expressed in spheres of light. What is being said here is that the knowledge of the universe, the secrets to understanding the reality of the cosmos, are within these spheres of light: they are units of energy that, when decoded, are the spiritual truth of all time. In other words, the light *is* the truth.

For me, this explains why many people at different times in the history of our world have had revelations about God and the universe that are in some ways similar and in some ways different. Ultimately, Divine Consciousness is beyond words and beyond what our human minds can comprehend. Most religious leaders and most mystics seem to agree that "light" is an important aspect of the Divine. It is hard to find a spiritual pathway that does not speak of light. But because truth contained within the light is beyond verbal language, it stands to reason that people who decode and translate the truth will not always come up with the same words or ideas.

The new thought for me is that the actual truths are *contained* within this light and that it comes to us in waves of an energetic form that we cannot, with any of our scientific instruments, measure at this time. I feel this light when I am in an altered state of consciousness. Even though I do not always see bright light, I sense that waves of light are pouring through me. All of a sudden, the light will become visible to my spiritual eyes, although it is not visible to my physical eyes.

Consider how I receive the teachings: I am a spirit who for the moment is clothed in a physical body. In other words, I am a living human being. As these waves of light come to me, they have to pass through that part of me that is spirit. While my conscious mind cannot receive these waves of light, during a channeling session, when I am in an altered state of consciousness, my spirit can receive this light and understand its message. The aspect of my spirit that is able to merge with Divine Consciousness is able to receive these teachings in the form of light, and then clothe these messages with human language. I then speak the messages as I have received and interpreted them.

I am not able to receive these teachings when I am in an everyday, go-to-the-grocery-store state of consciousness. I need to prepare myself for the channeling sessions by resting beforehand and then continue to prepare myself by allowing my conscious mind to step to the side, so that the spirit within, my Greater Self, can receive the teachings. The people with me must share my need for a sacred space and sacred spiritual environment. We create this sacred space with our intentions and our attitudes.

Where do the words come from? Are these my words? Yes and no. They are my words in the sense that my spirit has to receive the messages brought to me by the light and translate the messages into human language. If Chinese were my first language, the words would be Chinese; if Spanish were my first language, the words would be in Spanish. As English is my language, the words are in English. Yes, they are my English words, but, no, they are not the words I would speak when in a normal state of consciousness. I believe they are my words when I am in the highest state of consciousness I personally can achieve at this time; they are the words of my Greater Self, that part of me that, as a spark of the Divine, connects with Divine Consciousness. Each one of us is a spark of the Divine, and therefore, when any of us can merge with our Greater Selves, as we connect with Divine Consciousness, then wisdom can be communicated through us in that moment.

Where do the ideas come from? Are the words expressing my ideas? Again, yes and no. Yes, the ideas are clothed at times with images that my human mind can understand, such as, "Communication is like a long line of energy that flows from one to the other; it is like a wire, never ending, never broken, spiraling and twirling throughout eternity."

These words describe the energy in a manner that a human being can conceive of. We all understand what a line is; we all understand what a spiral looks like. Is the energy really a wire or a spiral? Maybe, maybe not. I am a human being living on the planet earth, so my Greater Self will come forward with the idea or image that I and others on this planet can understand. My Guidance is using my Greater Self to receive the energy, decode it, and translate it into language that human beings can comprehend. (I emphasize that it is my Greater Self that is able to receive this energy. In my everyday conscious mind, I do not receive such messages.)

On the other hand, if I were a totally different form of life from another planet or from a realm in the spirit world that we as human beings do not know about yet, I would receive the truths in a way that I and others like me could understand. In other words, the truth that is contained in the spheres of light and every life-form that merges with this truth expresses the truth in the kind of communication that is part of its own life-form. Think for a moment about the idea that the trees, mountains, oceans, rocks, and all forms of animals and plants have spirits. If this is true, the ocean would receive the truth in its own terms, and the birds would receive the truth in their own way.

Human beings respond and comprehend the truth depending on their level of spiritual evolution. What each one of us can learn from these "spheres of light" corresponds to the level of spiritual development we have or have not attained at a particular moment in time. In 1987, when I did my first channeling sessions, I was told that I was not ready for the sessions; the colors in my energy were not right, and I needed to work on improving my life and reducing my stress before coming back later. At that time I would not have been able to receive this light. By the first half of the 1990s, I was able to channel a portion of this light, and I learned a great deal from My Guidance. My Guidance communicated in the form of creative stories, poems, and rather homespun advice. In those years most of what came through seemed to be centered around myself and improving myself. And the advice worked. My relationships improved, I discovered that I was a psychic medium, and I started taking much better care of myself in all ways.

In the year 2004, when the Sitting Project began, I was more prepared to receive the light. Fifteen years or so ago, I do not believe I was ready to bring through the messages that are coming through today. I would not have been able to tolerate the intensity of the energy that is flowing through me today. I used to get nauseous and dizzy in the early days just bringing through poems and stories. Now I no longer have those physical irritations. For the most part, I am able to receive a deeper and more universal message without feeling so uncomfortable.

As the three of us sat and chatted after the December 15, 2005, session, it was clear that all of us were stunned by the messages that came through. Both Ron and Bob commented on how different the vibrations in the room were. We knew we had entered into an experience we had never anticipated. I came to realize more fully that My Guidance is really not mine at all, but a universal cosmic force.

January 8, 2006: Do Not Carry Extra Baggage

"The camel knows that the journey is long and that he will outlive many others who hurry, scurry, and worry."

Maui, one of the Hawaiian Islands, is one of the most beautiful and spiritual places in the world. I feel so fortunate that my parents moved to Maui, which has become my second home. I wrote the book you are reading, as well as *Heart and Sound* and *Consult Your Inner Psychic* in Maui, as the energy for writing is incredible.

Memories of the December 15, 2005, channeling session were still affecting me when I arrived in Maui in January 2006. How was my work with Spirit going to change now that my Greater Self had tapped into whole new cosmic realms? I was still mulling over the messages received in that session: "These messages are instant, and all of the universe is connected in a way that no one even has any inkling of yet." What did this mean?

I decided to do some solo channeling sessions, as I had done between 1987 and 1996. But I did not want to allow myself to go into as deep a state as I had been in when doing sessions with Ron and Bob back in Massachusetts. There was no one to protect me, no one to sense when it was time for me to come out. So I needed to take care of myself by restricting the depth of the trance state.

On my own with My Guidance, I found myself reverting back to the kinds of personal questions I used to ask during my solo days of channeling before the Sitting Project began. I said that I was worried that I was not good enough as a person, as a medium, or as a family member. What did My Guidance want to say to me about myself? As I look back, I realize that as I spoke about myself, I was looking for reassurance. I wanted compliments. I wanted my ego stroked! After expressing myself, I counted myself down into a slightly deep state and waited to hear the answer within my mind. The message that came through made it very clear that I was being asked to change—to mature.

MY GUIDANCE: Good morning, Carole, in answer to your question we are bringing you an image, again of the camel striding across the desert. Repeat the words as you hear them, and eventually there will be no time lag between what you are hearing and saying.

The camel strides across the desert patiently.

The camel is in for the long haul.

The camel cannot afford, in the heat in which it is walking, to waste any energy on nonsense.

The camel knows that the journey is long and that he will outlive many others who hurry, scurry, and worry.

You are the camel striding across the desert.

You must not carry extra baggage with you or you will not be able to make the journey.

You cannot worry about how long it is going to take you or the particular quality of each day, because the days are long and the distance is far that you are going.

The camel, through generations and generations of heredity, has learned this patience, this plodding motion.

You do not particularly come from a generation of patience, and we are bringing that to you from the world of spirit.

We are asking you to walk with us, to imagine yourself as the camel plodding across the desert.

And we are your companions as you walk slowly, steadily, and with great patience.

At times along the way there will be beautiful desert flowers, beautiful desert cactus that will give off aroma to boost your senses.

But on other days there will be nothing but barren sand and heat.

There will be nothing except your own internal self to carry your forward.

Stop looking for these flowers.

Stop looking for these special days.

Stop looking outside yourself.

Instead, look within, because that is where your serious patience and security lie.

That is where your strength is blossoming like a flower.

It is a flower so deep within that you cannot be boosted by the smell of its aroma at this point.

But it is the flower that is your strength.

It is the inner strength that you write about, that you talk about, and that you possess to a certain degree.

But in this next step in your journey, it is this inner strength that needs to increase and increase, and multiply and multiply, to a point where you are not asking questions like you needed to this morning.

We have compassion for your question because it is an earthly question.

It is a worry to be good.

It is a worry to be confident.

But these worries are taking energy from you that should be used now for spiritual development within yourself.

The camel strides in earthly fashion, but the patience comes from afar.

The patience comes from eons and eons back in the history of the world.

And ultimately that patience comes from God.

The camel, a very spiritual walk, is taken.

Model yourself after the camel.

Be the camel out in the desert.

There is a jewel within the camel.

If you look closely you will see the jewel within the solar plexus area, the stomach area of the camel and also in the third eye.

These jewels shine brightly within and keep the camel going

Dull you may say the camel looks.

But the camel is the power and the strength.

Comments

As I reflect on the ego-based questions I asked and the messages that came through for me, it is clear that the Divine wanted no part of my questions. I needed to realize it was time to move beyond worrying about myself. Suddenly, it was out of line to be merging with Divine Consciousness and asking, "Am I good enough?"

It is easy for many of us to be overly focused on ourselves. We become self-conscious about everything we do and worry a great deal about what others think, spending so much of our time and energy on impressing other people. We are raised in a culture that tells us we must be the best looking, the smartest, and the richest. Do we really want to spend our lives worrying and striving?

The next day I was given more advice on the management of my energy and in even more explicit terms.

January 9, 2006: Time to Grow Up

"You must like so many of the beautiful flowers:
after opening so wide, close."

MY GUIDANCE: Good morning, Carole. We are showing you a pin-point, and we are reminding you of one of your early channeling sessions that used the image of a pinpoint.

We asked you why you fly around the universe so much when it is a pinpoint that needs your attention.

Focus and attention are very important.

Your attention now is being drawn to your stomach. In a sense, this morning we are asking you to let your stomach be your guide.

You have always had very good instincts about what to do and what not to do.

We are pleased that you are working on your diet right now, because your attention does not need to be on food as much as it has.

We would like you to start consuming less food, whatever diet plan you are on, because the food and the digestion of this food is simply taking up too much of your energy.

You will feel much better when you are lighter.

It is not for the purpose of looks, which we know you value, but for the purpose of higher energy and more that you will be able to take in and give out in this world during the rest of your time in this life.

We do not want you to waste any more energy on temper flare-ups, depressions, anxieties.

You simply do not have time for that anymore.

What is being said is not critical, but you have had your time for all that.

And it is now time for you to walk the spiritual path of enlightenment, which does not respond to such energy.

We see a flower that has opened over many years; each petal that has opened slowly and with great purpose.

And now the flower is open and ready to give off its essence to all around.

But in order to do this, you must have protection.

You must like so many of the beautiful flowers: after opening so wide, close—close for the night, close for certain days.

You have the ability now to open and close as needed.

You will not need to go outside of yourself so much in the future as you have in the past.

While you will continue to have a couple of good confidantes with whom to bounce off ideas, you will not run to the wrong people anymore, confiding, as you have been doing.

The way you spend your time is going to have to change radically.

Go into your day now and do the things that you need to do.

Count up now . . .

Comments

In both the January 8 and 9 sessions, I received advice that would change my life. These messages speak to all of us on the spiritual path who want to be more trusting, patient, focused, and mature. As we contemplate the image of the flower, know that as we go deeper in our spiritual work, the flower's aroma is so deep within us that we should not expect to receive the fragrance all the time. We must have faith that the fragrance is there.

Like the flower, we exist in beauty and selflessness. We do not need anyone to compliment us or congratulate us. We will be absorbed in our spiritual work and not really aware of whether people approve of us or not.

Like the flower, we must protect our deep spiritual gifts by closing up. Aware of how we use our energy each day, we must be sure that we are energetically moving in the direction of spiritual development, spiritual awareness, and allowing spiritual guidance as we raise our consciousness to higher levels. Like the flower, we will bend toward the light. As we contemplate the image of the camel, we receive patience. We receive knowledge that some days on our journey are going to be better than others—some hot and dry, and others cooler, with more water available. We must stop asking for special days and experiences, but take what comes each day. Like the camel, we must be in for the long haul. Guidance will be with us as we walk our path.

As we walk the spiritual path, we will change. We will give up old habits. We will not be as focused on ego-centered worries. We will evolve. Like the flower, we will blossom. Like the camel, we will endure.

That week in Maui I realized that while I would still receive personal guidance, and perhaps an occasional compliment, from now on I was going to work with My Guidance in a new way, moving from the personal to the universal cosmic realm. As I look back on my solo sessions in Maui in 2006, I see that I was being kicked out of my ego-based habits and shot like a rocket into a whole new adventure.

Back to the Mainland: Walking on Ice

Late February brought me back to the Boston area, where I could not walk without fear of falling on the ice. What a comedown!

Thoughts were buzzing around my mind like busy bees. The early 1990s was such a time of transformation for me. Now it was 2006, and I was experiencing another cycle of death and rebirth.

One of the important steps I had taken in my life was to become an ordained minister in the religion of Spiritualism. I had worked hard for over seven years, taking courses in spiritual healing, mediumship, and the ministry. On April 26, 2003, I had been ordained in Plymouth, Massachusetts, by the American Federation of Spiritualist Churches. Spiritualism, the only religion I could be a member of and be a minister within, met me with open arms, accepting both my psychic and mediumistic gifts. Spiritualism did not dictate to me the ways I must think about God (who in Spiritualism is often called "Infinite Spirit" or "Infinite Intelligence"). My ordination was one more step in the process of giving my life over to the Divine. Now I was taking another step as I allowed my Greater Self to merge with Divine Consciousness to receive messages for us all. As a child, I had made a deal with God. Now I was keeping my part of the bargain. I was accepting my spiritual commitments on a much deeper level than ever before.

As each one of us discovers what our spiritual commitments are, and as we make choices that lead us in the direction of our commitments, we begin to give up some old habits, friends, and ways of spending our time. As we look back, we realize we have changed. The old self has died, and the new self has been born.

The Transition Sitting Project Sessions

During the first year that Ron and Bob started attending my channeling sessions, we all received personal guidance, and it was delivered in a more conventional way of speaking. During the years I had channeled by myself, the advice had typically come to me in the form of a story or poem. Even now, when I channel alone, the advice is expressed poetically.

The sessions the three of us attended in March and April of 2006 were the last sessions where we would receive much personal guidance. When I read the transcript of the session from March 9, it sounds like a group of friends receiving guidance from a teacher.

March 9, 2006: Steady Yourself

"It is the steadiness of your gait at this time
that will bring you to where you need to be."

In attendance:

Channel: Carole Lynne
Sitter: Ron Monroe
Sitter: Bob Blake

We were anxious to get together and sit for Spirit again. All three of us asked questions about our lives and received guidance. First, Bob asked questions about what he called his "wandering."

BOB: My general question that seems to relate to most of the things that I am now doing is that I seem to feel that I am wandering. And I realize that not all who wander are lost. But at the moment, I am feeling more lost, somewhat overwhelmed, and would appreciate any advice or guidance you would wish to share.

MY GUIDANCE: From our perspective, it is almost as if you will frighten yourself if you listen to some of your deeper thoughts. There are things that bother you that you do not want to cope with. You are not the kind of guy that likes messy things.

BOB: Yes.

MY GUIDANCE: We see your wandering as avoidance. As long as you are wandering and feeling lost, you can avoid looking at the changes you need to make in your life. We suggest that you stop thinking about wandering—that you stop thinking about yourself as being lost and instead write yourself a list of tough questions. You obviously like to write—that works for you. Use the process that you are comfortable with. Write down questions such as "What do I want?" "What is bothering me?" "What do I need to change in my life?" You may even wish to write a poem of inspiration and see what it means to you, and bring it back to us and talk about it with us.

BOB: I used to enjoy writing poetry and have not thought about that in this way.

Comments

We can all learn from the advice Bob received, as we have all felt lost at times. There comes a time to face whatever it is we are feeling and move on. Because Bob takes notes whenever he is in a session or class of any kind, writing things down would be good and very natural for him.

I've often said, "Thoughts are things, and they change our lives." If I imagine that I am shy, then I will behave as a shy person. If I imagine that I am very comfortable with people, then my behavior will be entirely different. In both cases, I live up to my image of myself.

Bob was told to change his image of himself. Like him, all of us can improve our lives by taking a close look at what we think of ourselves, and changing our self-images as needed.

Ron received advice in this session about his need to be "steady."

MY GUIDANCE: Ron, the word for you is *steady*. Steady, calm, methodical, plodding along, not trying to go too slowly or too fast. Not becoming too excited or depressed, too happy or too sad, but simply steady.

It is the steadiness of your gait at this time that will bring you to where you need to be.

All around you have been various explosions, and you will handle everything very well. But what you need to be is steady.

We are sending healing to your mother. She does not want to move very much right now.

RON: No, she doesn't.

MY GUIDANCE: Sitting and sitting—we find her staring more into space.

RON: Yes.

MY GUIDANCE: The name *Larry* is around your mother. Do you understand?

RON: I do know a Larry that is associated with my mother, yes.

MY GUIDANCE: Living.

RON: Yes.

MY GUIDANCE: We also feel someone in spirit with the name of Grace is trying to help her. It is not absolutely clear, as we speak, if this is an ancestor or some kind of Guidance.

RON: I know a Grace who would help my mother, yes.

MY GUIDANCE: A Grace in spirit.

RON: Yes.

Comments

In our sessions, Ron has often been advised to simplify his life and to generally calm down. This is good advice as Ron is a highly sensitive and easily excitable person.

It was good for all three of us to hear facts about Ron's mother's life, which I, as the channel, knew nothing about. Ron recognized the names Larry and Grace as belonging to people who are associated with his mother.

Again, we can all learn from the messages that Ron received. How often do we try to do things too quickly—for example, asking ourselves to accomplish in one month a job that will realistically take six months? We race around and damage the quality of our lives.

My Guidance also had some advice for me.

MY GUIDANCE: We see you as a piece of cheesecake crumbling on the plate right now. It is time for you to shape up. We know your energy is, in many ways, at its lowest, and we are trying to boost you. You are fighting many battles at the same time—to the right, to the left, to the front, to the back. It is really too much.

The boat is in the middle of the river. As it stays in the middle of the river, nothing can be accomplished. You have to keep rowing until you reach the other side.

The incredible exhaustion that you felt the other day, the sadness, and then your attempt to make yourself better, you ate things you should not have eaten, which is what caused all these blisters. Raisins, while they give you energy, are not the thing to eat for you when you are upset. And you ate so many of them. You are going to have to be very careful as to what you eat and drink in the next few months. There is much to be coped with, and you are not the kind of physical being who can cope with a lot of different kinds of foods. If you have to, carry a lunch box with you everywhere you go; you need to eat the foods that you know agree with you. No exceptions.

I do tend to eat the wrong foods and too much of them when I am upset. I am also quite sensitive to foods, and so when I do not eat properly, which for me means eating extremely carefully, I do not feel well. At this particular time, there were some problems in my life that I was trying to cope with in the wrong way. I was given good advice as I heard the words "No exceptions."

When I listened to the recording after the session, I was impressed with the words, "You have to keep rowing until you reach to the other side." At that time I was making some transitions in my life, and it was as if I were in the middle of the river, on neither one shore nor the other. I received a lot of strength from this advice.

All three of us received good advice in this session: Bob was told to just do things, and Ron was ironically told not to do so much, too fast. And I was told not to eat so much. All of the advice given to us centered around the need for us to find balance in our lives: not too much, not too little.

The Power of the Energy behind the Words

When words come through during a channeling session, it is not only the words, but also the energy contained within the words that is so powerful. None of the advice in this session was earth-shaking, but the energy we all felt within the room is hard to describe. It was cosmic and transforming.

Although we were getting help with our personal issues, Ron noticed that the energy was changing. Afterward he commented,

> This session was very different for me. Aside from seeing the usual sorts of energy formations that I have grown accustomed to seeing, the light and the different colors, I also felt that I was being used to help send you energy. I felt very strongly that I was being used in that way. Things got a little bit muddy for me, and I did not feel really conscious of what you were saying toward the end. I was only aware of this energy that was going from me to you.
>
> . . . I don't know if you felt it, but I saw what appeared to be a partial mask over your eyes—just a partial mask. Then when you spoke, or when Spirit was speaking of the color orange that they were sending to my mother for healing, your face got very orange.
>
> At least to my vision, it got extremely orange. Around the chest, I saw a blue energy. It was a deep blue energy that I was seeing. There were times when I felt as if I was seeing a force field; that is the only way I can describe it. You know how when you go into a force field and it shows those electrical impulses? I was seeing that kind of energy.

Bob commented after the session:

This did seem different; it did seem to be deeper. You did seem to be in a deeper state than you had before. I think you have commented, Carole, that as you feel Spirit coming to you, you start to move. I noticed that in this session, you were sort of accepting. You started to move back and forth. You were smiling. You were feeling something pleasurable. I could recognize the healing energy as you brought your hands up. I could recognize the healing posture. You did come forward. Unfortunately, I could not feel quite the same degree of heat the rest of you felt, but I did feel that the room got warmer. And when we talked about the temperature of the room at first, it was a little chilly here, and it did get warmed up. I felt more comfortable, and perhaps that's my way of feeling the difference in this session.

We were all grateful for the guidance that we had received in this fairly calm session. However, the next session would practically knock me off my seat.

April 3, 2006: A Symbol Becomes a Sound
"Om."

In attendance:
  Channel: Carole Lynne
  Sitter: Ron Monroe
  Sitter: Bob Blake

Much of this session was silent, so I will share an account of what happened during this unique experience.

It felt as if the spirit of a female shaman were superimposed over me. Ron saw vibrant colors, and Bob felt an intense energy. All of a sudden, I saw within my mind an image coming toward me. It was the symbol of *Om*, the Sanskrit syllable used as a mantra to connect with ultimate reality. As it got closer and closer, the part of me that is conscious got nervous. Within, I started crying out, "What is going to happen?" Then an incredible wave of energy came over me and seemed to jolt the spirit of the female shaman right out of my consciousness. Suddenly, I was in deep trance state and the sound of *Om* was coming out of my mouth. I did not feel as if I was singing. It felt like the energy of *Om* was singing through me.

After the session, Ron was very excited. He commented, "It was very abrupt—bang, the energy changed, and it felt like a different energy came in. And I found myself wondering what was happening. I had this sense of a couple of things happening simultaneously. I could feel a healing vibration coming forward."

I was in awe of the power I had felt coming toward me while I was in trance. The image of the *Om* symbol was so real, so vivid, and seemed to contain the power of the universe. When both the image and the sound merged with me, I literally felt the spirit of the woman who was communicating through me being thrown out of my consciousness. It reminded me of the séance scene in the movie *Ghost,* when the spirit of a man suddenly took over Whoopi Goldberg's body and then suddenly left her. When I look back on this experience, there is a humorous side, but at the moment it was not funny.

When the sound of *Om* began to sing itself through me, I lost a sense of myself as a human being and as a channel for Spirit as my entire being merged with this beautiful sound. It was one of those experiences that I would never try to repeat; one cannot place an order with the spirit world for such an experience as one orders a meal in a Chinese restaurant. The sound was an unexpected gift that I received with gratitude.

After the session, all three of us felt as if we had experienced a spiritual healing. It was a beautiful session and a wonderful event in our lives.

May 4, 2006: We Are All One and Yet We Are Many

"Because you have five senses, it is logical for you to think in terms of what you see, what you hear, what you smell, and your senses have led you to dividing things up in a way that for us in not relevant."

In attendance:
Channel: Carole Lynne
Sitter: Ron Monroe
Sitter: Bob Blake
Guest: Brenda Lawrence, MSNU

Meet Our Guest: Brenda Lawrence, MSNU

I met Brenda when I took courses for many years at the Arthur Findlay College. Brenda is not only a wonderful medium who travels around the world giving demonstrations of spirit communication, but she is also an incredibly smart and sensitive teacher. I was very fortunate to have her take me under her wing in the early days of my mediumship development. Brenda is also a minister who gives of her time to those in need, and she is extremely respected by all who work with her.

Brenda has been the perfect teacher for me, because she avoids a cookie-cutter approach to spiritual development. She knows that individuals develop in their own way. In the early years of my work with her, she told me that while I was always going to work as a medium and bring people messages from their loved ones in spirit, there would come a time when I would expand and add other kinds of spiritual work into my life. Now, in 2006, I was about to have the opportunity to share my expanding spiritual experience with my teacher, but I have to admit I was a bit nervous about it.

Brenda has been sitting for trance for many years and has regular sitters who work with her. When she goes into a deep state, she is aware of the particular guides who are working through her. I did not know how Brenda would feel about the energy that came through me because it has never appeared to be the spirit of an individual who lived a life on earth.

The following is a partial transcript of our May 4, 2006, session.

CAROLE LYNNE IN HER OWN VOICE: I will repeat the words that I hear and after a while there will be no time lag.

(Ron slowly counts down from ten to one as I move into the trance state.)

MY GUIDANCE: Good evening.

We come from a very different place—a place not known to the channel. We're from a place of energy not known to many, certainly not to the channel. We are not in the form of human beings, as you would think of human forms. We are not your so-called space aliens either. If you wanted to draw a picture of us, you would not be able to. We are not like that.

We are like streams of energy—streams of knowledge in the universe. And you cannot personify us in the way that you would like to.

We are born out of each other. I say "each other" because that is a way that you can understand it. But it is as if one of us or one of the streams of energy is going along and then it may divide by two, going in slightly different directions. And then those two streams

Cosmic Connection

may divide again. Sometimes the energy comes back and it goes back to the hole from where it started, and other times it continues on into infinity. As it moves along, it picks up things along the way.

You think that you are learning from us, but we are also learning from you. As our energetic strands weave in and out of your earth, and out of many other places in the universe, we are picking up as much as we are leaving off.

Each time the knowledge keeps growing and is multiplied. Sometimes we hit what your Stephen Hawking would call a "black hole." We get lost for a while.

The channel is having trouble bringing through my words as she feels this is a great science fiction. But I am telling you that it is our truth.

We cannot influence the weather like you might think we can. We have nothing to do with the weather—whether you have storms or hurricanes or any of that. In fact, we can't influence much at all. All we can do is learn and give our information to those who can absorb our energy, and also learn from you.

Some people do not realize the way that we are imparting energy to them. We bring a thought into their minds, and they do not quite know where it comes from. Or two people might be walking down the street and one glances at the other, and for the moment, their eyes meet, and they don't know each other. And there is this soulful look that happens. Sometimes we are part of that. We are part of the energy between people. We love matchmaking. We love putting souls together and helping people be drawn to those that are good for them.

What questions do you have about us?

BRENDA: You say that you are energy. How may we perceive the energy?

MY GUIDANCE: You who live on earth often perceive what you call vibrations. The vibrations of your sound waves, the vibrations of your light waves—that is the usual way for you to perceive our energy. There are no instruments yet invented that can measure our energy as it exists.

RON: As I have been sitting here and observing, I have been drawn to what appears to be color around the channel. Are you a part of that color that I am seeing? Is that a way that you are able to cause me to perceive you?

MY GUIDANCE: Not really, because the colors that you see are the colors in the aura of the channel. We are going to need to rearrange her for a moment because she is extremely uncomfortable. Give us a second.

(Pause in the dialogue)

MY GUIDANCE: The colors that you see around the channel are the colors from her guides and those that work with her and from her own aura. But we are a different energy, and you would not see us in the usual colors, even the spiritual colors that you see.

BRENDA: Have the guides facilitated in this communication?

MY GUIDANCE: The guides have to be there in order for us to be able to transmit to her and through her, because our energy is a little bit different. And so, in your terms, her guides almost act as transformers. And this explains something for her, because she has always known that there is this energy around her, but then there are also these guides, and (she) has never before realized the relationship.

BOB: Do you also imply that this constant stream of energy that is picking up and leaving (missing words here)?

MY GUIDANCE: No, that is not how it works. As we said in the beginning, we are a stream of energy, and there are many streams that divide and multiply and go in different directions, picking up knowledge from those that we interact with and giving knowledge to those we interact with. But as far as the birth-and-death process, that is not what we are involved in.

BRENDA: What knowledge do you assimilate that you wish to share?

MY GUIDANCE: We are trying to understand the tones of human beings, because we find so many different variations that it is hard for us to understand how they all could be called human beings. Why is one so totally different from the other? Sometimes it is explained by many in your world as reincarnation and that people have different paths. We are trying to understand what it is that makes one so different from the other. We are not sure, but this is one of our main studies. And as we interact with you, we are trying to nudge you, we are trying to break through some of the walls that you have so that you will start to see the higher parts of your consciousness. In fact, we can only interact with the very highest part of your individual soul consciousness. But for those who do not open their minds, they will never feel our presence. We feel that those who open their hearts and their minds so that we may interact with them will become kinder people. Does that answer your question?

BRENDA: If you think about different tones of human beings, do we each have our own particular song or rhythm that our soul sings to us?

MY GUIDANCE: From your perspective, we divide these vibrations up into different things that you call waves and sound and colors and all. But to us, it is all one and the same—an energy perceived through different lenses at different times. And yes, you each have your own imprint. That is the best way that I can put it: your own vibrational imprint that may express itself through a tone or through a color. But I can't say that you are each a particular tone or song.

BOB: Perhaps we each have our own tonal signature in the same way that is recognizable which would allow you to see differences in us.

MY GUIDANCE: We see it as a vibrational pattern. Using the word *see* is not quite right. It is an essence. It is a particular essence—vibrational essence. We do not have it divided up as you do. Because you have five senses, it is logical for you to think in terms of what you see, what you hear, what you smell, and your senses have led you to dividing things up in a way that for us is not relevant. That is not to say that there is anything wrong with the way you have divided it up. It is just not relevant for us. It's just different.

RON: When you speak of the number of yourselves, when you use the word *we*, what do you mean? Is there any way that you are divided, or are you all part of the same emanation?

MY GUIDANCE: It is very hard to describe. We are all one and yet we are many. We don't have personalities as you do. We are vibrational streams of knowledge. There is no way to compare it to your individuals. Using the word(s) *we are* does not really express it. We are a stream of energy that is as ancient as time. We have divided and split up and gone in many directions, and at the same time that we are in many directions, we are also all joined by our impulses.

The only thing that I can think of that would relate to the way that some people on earth are beginning to think of is quantum physics with its bilocation, where something can be in the same place and another place at the same time. It is not quite like that, but that is the only thing that begins to approach our being, our reality.

RON: It seems like our theory of bilocation is far less advanced from what you know.

MY GUIDANCE: Not necessarily—just different. The channel has always perceived us as an energy rather than an entity. We are explaining to her for the first time what this is like, what this energy is like.

It is extremely old energy, yet it is constantly energized by all the centuries that it has come through. Do you understand?

(Ron and Bob say something to each other that cannot be understood.)

BOB: Because of the nature of what you say you are, our centuries must seem mere seconds to you.

MY GUIDANCE: Not really. We have a kind of sense of time. It is not like your sense of time. We go back and forth within time. We don't just move forward. We also move backwards, some of us.

BOB: Then is it somewhat random? Or can you choose your direction?

MY GUIDANCE: We are attracted—we are attracted by various things that are happening and to various people. Where we feel impressed that there is knowledge to be shared, we go. So it is as much up to you who are living and those who are in different life-forms in the universe to attract us. We are not controlling it, but we are attracted to you. There is a mutual exchange that is beneficial.

That's why people have so many different talents. We can aid in people's talents. We did not create them. We are attracted to an engineer, say, and we can go and help with that engineering project, help with that invention, or that poem or that song.

What do you see as you look at the channel?

BRENDA: A deep green. I sense a stream of energy that is like sometimes when you look at dust motes in the light. I can see it.

MY GUIDANCE: What do you see?

RON: I have been observing a number of different shifts in the energy around the channel. In the very beginning I saw what I have come to know as the colors of the channel's guide, superimposed over her chest. I have seen that energy move to the right shoulder area. I see a shift in the energy around the face of the medium as well. I have also seen what appeared to be a shaft of light in front of the medium.

I need to talk about the cold that I felt on my lower legs and across my lap. As I sat here, that energy was very constant. I felt the heat, as well, on the upper part of my body.

MY GUIDANCE: What do you see?

BOB: I see mainly physical changes, such as different transformation of the facial features, shadow across the face.

MY GUIDANCE: We are going to reorganize.

(Occasionally, in a session I will become terribly uncomfortable because I have been sitting in a fixed position for a long time. When this happens, My Guidance may take a moment to reorganize. When that happens, I may shift my physical position slightly and then go back into a deep trance state. In this case, not only did I change positions, but My Guidance also told us that the nature of the session was changing.)

MY GUIDANCE: We are bringing in healing energies. I would like each of you to receive a healing.

To Ron . . . (Healing was sent first to one and then the other, until all in the room had received healing. There is no more speaking.)

Comments

When I am in an altered state of consciousness, which many would call trance, part of my mind remains active and I can hear what is going on. As I spoke the words, my mind saw an image of the sources of energy that went along as one, divided, and became many more. It was as if mystical spiders were spinning a web of knowledge around the sitters and me. I got the impression that this web of knowledge was something that moves through the whole world and through all the universes that exist.

I have to admit, and My Guidance even commented on it, that at times I felt as if I were creating a great science fiction story. While my conscious mind finds it hard to believe that "[i]t is extremely old energy, yet it is constantly energized by all the centuries that it has come through," another, deeper part of me—the part of my Greater Self that is able to receive this energy— knows this statement to be true.

All of us were incredibly intrigued by what My Guidance said and by what we had felt. My Guidance taught us that the energy that comes through is ancient and cosmic and that it is both teaching us and learning from us. As the energy moves through the universe, there is a mutual exchange of knowledge.

This insight makes me think about the story of the "Hundredth Monkey Effect," which originated with Lyall Watson in his 1979 book *Lifetide*. In the story, a monkey learns a particular behavior. Then several other monkeys, upon observing this one monkey, also learn the behavior. The point at which 100 monkeys have learned the new behavior is a tipping point; now monkeys all over the world adopt the same behavior even though they have not observed the first monkey or the next ninety-nine. I wonder if this Energy plays a role in picking up knowledge *from one monkey* and dropping it off *with another*. This Energy may be the energy of knowledge that travels on its own without the assistance of our human vocabulary, printed pages, faxed documents, or FedEx packages filled with all kinds of information.

By the time we had reached the end of the May 4 session, I noticed that all of us were occasionally using the name "the Energy" instead of "My Guidance." We were seeing the many layers, the many aspects, of what I had called "My Guidance." My Guidance was no longer mine, but was now for me, and for us, the Energy.

I feel blessed that part of my Greater Self is able to connect with the Energy, receiving waves of vibrational teachings and translating them into words for the four of us and for all of humanity to contemplate. However, never will I fool myself into thinking that the words are the teachings; words are only words, and ultimately the Energy is wordless.

July 31, 2006: We Are Connections

". . . We are not Jesus. We are not Mohammad.
We are not any of those spiritual leaders because we
have never lived a human life. And yet you know
that we are there when you open to the presence."

In attendance:

 Channel: Carole Lynne
 Sitter: Ron Monroe
 Sitter: Bob Blake

Note: from this point on in the session transcripts, My Guidance is referred to as the Energy.

The following is a partial transcript of the July 31, 2006, session.

THE ENERGY: We are here to talk about whatever you would like this evening.

We are the same energy as before. We know that you and the channel have many questions about our essence, and so we will let you ask.

RON: There are lots of questions that need answers. I know that you explained that you are not anything that we know. My mind has a little bit of trouble processing what that means. Is there another way you can help us understand what you are?

THE ENERGY: We do not exist in any way in the same realm that you do. You are looking for identification and personification that we simply do not have in the same way that you do. We do not even speak. It is by a process that we are able to send impressions into the mind of the channel who can then put it into words. If we were to have a Japanese channel, the channel would be speaking Japanese. Do you understand?

We are an energy. We are a stream of light. We are a speck of energy that then explodes and becomes many more. We are not people. We are not creatures. We are energy, vibration. To use the word *we* does not really work.

Think about how the universe was formed. It was formed out of an explosion of energy. Can you understand that?

RON AND BOB: Yes.

THE ENERGY: We have been there since that very beginning. We're the nexus of what happened. But again to use words that you use does not really describe who we are. We are creative energy. We are what comes to you and helps you think of things. You feel our presence, and you know that we exist, but you can't prove it.

RON: When we began this evening, I felt an energy come in. I felt a presence that I could not define. Do I understand correctly that you are helping me formulate ideas in my mind?

THE ENERGY: This is the energy you draw on when you are inspired. The presence that you felt, the channel felt. In fact, she became so overwhelmed with the presence that she did not know if she could go on. We had to tone down her feelings.

We are not just with her. We are everywhere. We are creative energy; we are sustained imagination and creativity.

BOB: And yet as I remember you are different from what we think of as spirit.

THE ENERGY: Yes.

Now we are into words, because when you think of spirit, most human beings think of the spirit of this person and of that person— of spirits that lived once. And then you speak of Great Spirit, which is the god of your understanding. We are closer to the god of your understanding than we are to the spirit of your grandmother or grandfather or spirit guides. We are not spirit guides in the way that you think of it.

BOB: But in the sense of your earlier comment, that were you talking to Japanese people right now, their conversation would be in Japanese. So we must use our frame of reference when we think of spirit, and think of the closeness of the human form that we were used to, and that as they go into a form of energy, the only thing we can do to sort of accept that, I guess, is to use the same words that we attribute to that energy, the characteristics that we knew when they were here. That is a comfort to us, and it helps in our understanding and acceptance of the process we call death.

THE ENERGY: Of course it does, and that is very valuable. It is just not what we are. We are no better. There is not a contest here.

BOB: I understand. There is not a qualitative process.

But in the sense then that you, an energy, existed when the universe began, it seems that the energy from which you came subsequently formed into different parts that we are just beginning to discuss with you. Apparently, some parts of that original energy stayed as energy and became—and I will use our word—the entity that you are discussing, which equates to you and is still energy, while other parts of that original energy went off in a different direction and resulted in the evolution of what we call human, and the spirit that ignites that human presence.

Is that a fair statement? Perhaps more naïve?

THE ENERGY: It is not a matter of being naïve. It is that we are such a different realm it is hard to put it across in your frame of reference. We send an essence of this to the channel, and we have to bring it through her mind. But it cannot really be described in your terms.

If you can try not to personify the Energy, you will be closer to what it is.

BOB: As you said that, it occurred to me that the best thing we can do is accept that we cannot describe you, nor should we try, and instead, recognize that you are something that is beyond our understanding but which we know is there because there is a presence coming through the channel. So it seems acceptance is the right way to proceed rather than trying to fulfill our curiosity to learn more about it. In my case, I think it would take a significantly greater education, perhaps in physics and things I know very little about, and I would still come to the point where we are now of acceptance that you are there, you are communicating with us, and the how is not important. It is, however, important and significant to us that we are able to be a part of your communication and enjoy that as it is.

THE ENERGY: When you walk into the garden and you see a beautiful pink flower and you stop, there is a moment where time seems to stop because of the beauty. We are surrounding that flower. We are drawing you to it. We are connections. We are interconnections. And when we are there, you know we are there because you feel a presence. Something is different.

In your terms, you could say, it is the presence of spirit. But you cannot personify it. There are many great spiritual leaders that have lived that were people that survive in spirit. But that is not who we are. We are not Jesus. We are not Mohammad. We are not any of those spiritual leaders because we have never lived a human life. And yet you know that we are there when you open to the presence.

Comments

My Guidance had become the Energy. It was as if My Guidance took off a costume I had created and was showing me its true nature. I still continued to use both names, My Guidance and the Energy, just as I sometimes call people in my family by several different names.

We began to understand that the Energy is not an essence we can personify and classify. As Ron, Bob, and I were human beings, it is hard to conceive of an energy that was not a spirit who had lived on earth expressing itself to us through my channeling. The three of us accepted that when human life is over, our spirits live on in an eternal world, and when we communicated with that world, we expected to see images in our minds of our loved ones who have passed on. We also expected guidance in the form of spirit guides, angels, or helping spirits. We also thought about a loving god who is superior to all of our relatives in spirit and our spiritual guides. We thought about a god who can control the weather, birth, and death. It was hard for us to cope with the idea that the Energy I channeled was none of the above, and I can imagine it would be downright impossible for a person who does not at least believe in life after death to cope with it.

As I listened to the tape of the session, I was touched by Bob's expression of acceptance. Sometimes all of us have spiritual experiences that are special to us, that are life changing and transforming. When we try to explain these experiences and prove their validity, we often lose the mystical essence of the experience. I am sure many readers can relate to times of transformation when there was no explanation. Sometimes trying to put the experience into words causes the spiritual energy to instantly evaporate. Acceptance is often the best path.

When the butterfly is before you, accept its beauty. When the moon is full, bask in its light. When the warm waves of the ocean lap at your feet, accept the healing.

October 10, 2006: What Is *I* Amongst All of That?

"The physical life that you lead is the physical life that
you lead, but there is also this other realm
going on at the same time within you."

In attendance:

Channel: Carole Lynne
Sitter: Ron Monroe
Sitter: Bob Blake
Guest: Nora Shaw, MSNU

Meet Nora Shaw, MSNU

You may remember Nora Shaw from chapter 1. She is the teacher whose words changed my life. "If a medium can do an evidential reading, and bring evidence that she is in touch with your Uncle or Aunt or another of your loved ones, evidence that she does not have any knowledge of, and therefore prove beyond any doubt that she is communicating with your loved one in spirit, then it is also quite possible that when this same medium feels that she is bringing through wisdom from a spiritual Source, that she is." Nora has worked with the Spiritualist National Union for many years as a medium, teacher, and written-course instructor. She has worked all over the world and spends a great deal of her time working in England and Wales. Many note her to be one of the nicest and most spiritual people anyone could ever meet, and I can vouch for that! She has a lyrical and almost magical tone of voice, and I can receive knowledge from her simply by receiving the energy of her voice on the telephone. Even better is the opportunity to be in her presence. Just being with her brings a sense of healing.

The following is a partial transcript of our October 10, 2006, session, for which Nora was in attendance.

RON: In the past we have worked with an energy that describes itself as moving and fragments of light that pick up knowledge and impart knowledge but is not a person.

BOB: I believe we are here for the purpose of trying to communicate with higher beings such as yourself, and I use the word *being* because it is my sense, my perception. We have been in communication with an entity which describes itself as an energy which travels the universe and is attracted to people and places where there is knowledge to be shared. It has indicated a curiousness to learn more about us as well as trying to satisfy our curiosity as to what it is and what it represents.

The Sitting Project

We appreciate the opportunity to be in your presence as you join us for this group, but at the same time, we are always interested in the channel in particular: Is there more to this purpose than we have suggested in the past? Do you have a sense of what our purpose is jointly?

THE ENERGY: You have understood what we have been trying to say in past sessions.

And we want you to understand that this energy is as much a part of the minerals of the earth—the rocks, the ocean—as it is of anything else. People in human bodies continually want to think of intelligence in their own form, but true intelligence is not limited to a personified human existence. Can you understand that?

BOB AND RON: Yes.

THE ENERGY: What we are talking about here is an intelligence that moves through nature, that moves through the universe. And it also moves through you. And we welcome Carole's teacher tonight. Welcome to you.

(At this point in the session the Energy begins to give us a cosmic grammar lesson: do *not* use pronouns.)

THE ENERGY: So before we can really proceed, the idea of a "you," of a "we," of an "I," of a "me," as any kind of personified being has to be let go of as it is very difficult for us to converse. You are doing very well and beginning to let go of this, but it is asked that you let go of this concept even more because that is the only way that you can understand this energy that is flowing through the channel. And what is even more important is not so much that you understand what is flowing through Guidance as you understand what is flowing through each one of you. What you are hearing is just the energy flowing through one person, but there is no monopoly on this energy by anyone.

How do you respond to that thought?

BOB: I understand that, and my feeling is that over the last few sessions it has been different to think of an energy in a pure form as pure energy without form. And I think, at this point, I am used to that and look forward to having this communication as translated through the channel.

RON: For me, it is really becoming part of my everyday reality to understand something about the nature of communicating forces: that they are not always discarnate beings that are communicating with us. I am beginning to understand that I receive information from many different things, including the rocks, the trees, and the plant and animal life. I am beginning to see this thread of intelligence that permeates everything, but has no shape or no mind as we would consider it.

THE ENERGY: It has no mind as you would consider a human mind, but it does have an intelligence that is mindlike. And you understand that if this energy flows through the channel, she has to put into her own words because we do not even speak in words. We do not speak; we are not "we."

It is more important that you feel within yourself this energy as it flows through you than you understand what we are saying, because to try to understand this on an intellectual level is impossible.

So what are your questions this evening? The three of you.

RON: We opened by speaking about the energy that is present this evening, that hasn't been here before. I am a little bit curious about this energy and its purpose in being here this evening.

THE ENERGY: There is a lifting of the vibration of the energy that is a combination of all four human beings in the room. It is a bit brighter, a bit lighter. The channel sees a great deal of light even though the room is dark.

Does that answer your question?

GROUP: Yes.

(At this point in the session, Ron begins to ask the Energy questions about healing. The subject of spiritual healing is very important to everyone in our group, including our guest Nora. In a number of previous sessions, messages about healing have come through, and these messages said that the main purpose of the Sitting Project is, ultimately, to heal the members of the group. In this next exchange between Ron and the Energy, a lot is said about the role of the soul in a human being in need of healing.)

RON: We have talked about the purpose that the Energy has in respect to healing. I am wondering what the purpose is. Does the Energy have anything that it would like to expand upon in respect to working with each of us through healing? Previously, we have discussed the healing of each individual within the group.

THE ENERGY: The healer works with the person in need. The energy that comes through the healer simply announces to the ones receiving the healing that healing is available. But it is the soul receiving the healing that makes the decision as to what form the healing is going to take. The soul receiving the healing knows if it is time to go back home to eternal life or whether it is time to recover from the symptoms. But all the healer is doing is providing an environment and a setting so that the energy can flow through and say that healing is available. But it is the soul of the individual that decides how that healing is to go and how it will manifest.

From our point of view, too much emphasis has been put on the healer and the energy coming through the healer that is going to somehow do something to the one in need. But that is not how, from our energetic perspective—that is not what happens. Again, the healer creates an environment, and in a sense it is like knocking on the door and saying, "Hello, healing is at the door."

RON: What you say suggests there could be a disparity between what the soul feels is appropriate in respect to a healing situation and what the incarnate mind wants.

(The cosmic grammar lesson is in full swing now.)

THE ENERGY: First of all, lets get rid of the word *you*. Can we do that? I will get rid of the word *we*.

RON: That is going to be hard, but we'll try.

THE ENERGY: Let's try. And let's get rid of "the soul feels."

The best words that we can put to it are that "the soul knows its destination." The soul knows whether it is time to go home to the eternal life of the spirit or it is time to heal from the symptoms that are present at the moment. Whatever is in the mind of the healer or in the mind of the individual with the symptoms is of little consequence. Because that is all on a level of the personality, and the soul, which is connected to the Divine Energy, is in a different realm: Very difficult to put this into language.

RON: I have a sense of it. It is hard for me to separate out the *we*, etc., but I have a sense of it.

THE ENERGY: Say, "There is a sense of it."

RON: There is a sense of it, yes.

THE ENERGY: Rather than "I have a sense of it," "there is a sense of it."

Anyone else?

BOB: It seems like the more we get used to the idea that there is no *we*, that we are all energy, the easier it becomes to consider that concept. At the same time, it is as though our forms, bodies, which include the various processes in our brain, are somewhat limited by being used to the brain as a filter, which causes us not to fully understand what comes through or tells us that we are seeing certain information for the first time in our conscious mind. It sounds as though the energy that is a part of all of us is there, but most of us deal on a more physical or more superficial plane, and it takes some work on our part to get rid of the pronouns and understand that all is.

THE ENERGY: Lift up into a different consciousness and perceive the vibration within. When you speak about "we do this and we do that, and it is hard for us," it drags you into a realm where you cannot perceive. So use different words. Allow the energy within to flow into a different realm, and you will perceive. Or all will perceive.

BOB: Perhaps it is that same process which is holding me back right now—the physical me that is stuck right now and wondering how to proceed.

THE ENERGY: Do not think "stuck." Thinking stuck equals stuck. Leave it.

BOB: Very well.

THE ENERGY: The place to start is different language.

RON: There seems to be a sense of an intermingling of energies in which there is no separation, in which everything is a part.

THE ENERGY: Where all is one, there is no need for intermingling, as there is nothing to intermingle with anything else. Intermingling is still not what it is.

BOB: It seems, then, that the purest form of communication, of interaction, is that of experiencing, and our difficulty is in being limited to communicating with words. If we could use telepathy, or if we could just experience one another, that would be a purer, faster, more comprehensive way to communicate and understand.

THE ENERGY: Do not confuse modes of understanding with vibration, with the physical life you must lead every day. The physical life that you lead is the physical life that you lead, but there is also this other realm going on at the same time within you. It is not to give up your personality, your physical way of being. It is a matter of a glimpse into a different realm if you want that glimpse.

Does our guest have any questions?

NORA: I am just observing. Thank you. One comment: I think that—and I shouldn't use the word *I* or *we*—but we spend a lot of time analyzing instead of learning.

THE ENERGY: Well put, and learning is?

NORA: The beginning of understanding.

THE ENERGY: Learning is the beginning of understanding.

Can you appreciate why we need to get rid of *you, we, I* words as we try to learn?

NORA: Yes, we can. Learning acceptance without question.

RON: As I think about using those words, I feel a sense of the boundaries that are set up. By using all of these pronouns, our minds are kept from expanding as we remain in an old pattern of thinking. Bob used the word *stuck*.

THE ENERGY: These boundaries are necessary as you go to fill your car with gas, and go to the supermarket to buy a piece of chicken. There is nothing wrong with the boundaries, but when there is a time for learning, experiencing a different consciousness, there is no place for those boundaries in that moment. One state of consciousness is no better than the other—just different.

Human beings always seem to want to say that there is something wrong with the everyday way of being. That is not true.

The energy is the energy. Very few human beings are even remotely interested.

Anything else?

RON: I am trying to get rid of these pronouns. I am trying to allow my mind to expand far beyond what I am currently able to perceive. I do not know if I am making myself clear.

The Energy: You were until you said, "I do not know if I am really making myself clear."

NORA: Yes.

(The cosmic grammar lesson continues. In the next dialogue, the sitters are corrected when they use a pronoun and encouraged to speak in a more universal language. The Energy is trying to get the sitters to stop using pronouns such as *I, you, we, they* and *me* and to show the group how different the vibration or energy is within the room when thoughts are delivered in a more universal kind of language. If "all is one," then there is no need for *you, I, we, they,* or *me.*)

THE ENERGY: Could you not feel the difference in vibration when you interjected that last statement?

RON: Yes, I could.

THE ENERGY: So stay in the energy you were in and just see what you say. Or what is said. Continue.

RON: So for me—

THE ENERGY: No.

RON: No, I am going to try to stay in this energy.

This higher vibration gives a sense that, as was stated earlier, there really is only one. There really is only one.

(At this comment, which Ron expresses without using any pronouns, we all feel a change in the energy within the room.)

THE ENERGY: All is One. We feel the energy of it even on a personality level: All is One.

RON: On a very minor level, there is a sense of it, yes.

THE ENERGY: And Bob.

BOB: It is still difficult to let go of the boundaries we have in this physical being, to get to complete understanding.

THE ENERGY: Good.

BOB: The logic that I used—that is used—seems to be a formidable barrier to the letting go that is suggested.

THE ENERGY: Logic is a formidable barrier; however, it is not a letting go. It is an expansion. If you focus on what you need to let go of, you will simply hang on to it. Do not think of it. Expand—just expand.

BOB: Understood.

THE ENERGY: The energy is going to become too much for the channel fairly soon, so if there are additional questions . . .

BOB: The channel is interested in whether or not she should be doing more writing.

THE ENERGY: We do not know things like that. One who wants to write, writes. As has been said in other sessions, this energy, this vibration, has no instructions and no control. So while we appreciate her question, it is irrelevant.

BOB: Understood. And perhaps had the question been considered, had we been aware of the substance of your last comment before the question was thought of, there would have been no need for such a question.

THE ENERGY: Good.

Those in this room have chosen to come together. The energy that is flowing through the channel is what is happening at this time. The purpose is knowledge and expansion. Thank you for your questions.

RON: Thank you for your answers.

THE ENERGY: It is time to start bringing the channel out.

(Ron slowly counts from one to ten.)

Comments

The messages in this session taught us that we are not separated. We are all part of the same energy. The Energy felt that one way for us to experience the nature of the Energy was to speak in a more universal language that did not include pronouns.

As we all sat around chatting after the session, the subject of "collective consciousness" came up.

Ron commented that he felt an expansion when he avoided using pronouns. He had felt a bit of a freedom and said that if we allowed ourselves to be in that space it could be extremely freeing.

I said that we had all had a little glimpse into this wordless sphere.

Then Nora commented:

The kind of thing that the mystics, the true mystics, touch on (is that) they reach a point of heightened experience, heightened consciousness, where they are just part of the universe or they feel they have experienced God or imagined God's face. So a true mystic will reach that level where there isn't any personality and where it's just being absorbed. And for the Buddhist, it is being absorbed in Nirvana. There is a tribute to Jesus, and he says, "I and My Father are One."

We talk a lot about the collective consciousness and that we can all access that collective consciousness—that ever was, ever will be, all of that knowledge.

And of course we think of it as being consciousness that is human, because we think of man being the reasoning animal and *egotistically set those parameters, overlooking or even disregarding the sensitivity in all of creation, however limited we deem some aspects of that to be* I think that collective consciousness has got to be part of everything *animal, vegetable and even mineral.* And then it makes sense to not say *I* because what is *I* amongst all of that?

And recognizing that although we are important, we are totally unimportant. We always want to associate personality with this is so-and-so, this is Joe Bloke communicating. We don't question and say, "Who are you?"

We accept what he has given and not the source.

When Nora spoke to us about the collective consciousness, there was a power behind her words that rocked the whole room. In fact, I literally had to leave the room. I was overwhelmed.

Many of you have experienced moments in your life when the truth is spoken. While you may have even heard the words before, in that moment, the Truth behind the words and filling the words is pure transformative power. It is the Energy within the words, behind the words, that contains the Truth. The words are but vehicles. The flower standing by itself in the sunshine is perhaps a better vehicle for the Truth than any words. The flower is giving, selfless, and utterly beautiful. When Nora spoke about the collective consciousness, the power of her words contained the essence of the most beautiful flowers in the world.

August 13, 2007: Spirit Wraps Us in a Cocoon

*"We are almost ready for some sessions with no words.
Not today, not soon. As the three of you sit, you are learning
to hold this energy. You are absorbing it. It is affecting you.
You have only to think back a couple of years and
all of you will note that you have changed in some way."*

In attendance:
Channel: Carole Lynne
Sitter: Ron Monroe
Sitter: Bob Blake

During the first few minutes of the session, I was able to speak in my own voice. Then, once in a deeper state, I repeated the words

I heard within my mind and within seconds, there was no time lag between what I was hearing and what I was saying.

CAROLE LYNNE STILL IN HER OWN VOICE: I feel that I need to report that I feel spirit influence trying to overshadow me. I felt a presence on my eyelids, and then I felt my lips start to swell, but I am asking those spirit influences not to come through me this evening, because I would like to channel the Energy that I have been channeling.

Please count from ten to one.

RON: I feel a little bit of a temperature change around the lower portion of my legs. It feels as though it is now hot in the room, in spite of the fact that my legs feel cold.

BOB: Because we are slightly warmer, other than the physical movements of the medium, I don't notice anything else. There seems to be a little movement back and forth, left to right, and as her head came up, there seems to be a concerned look on her face as if she is trying to focus on something.

RON: Periodically, I am also aware of the energy around her body, I would call the etheric body, but also I feel a little bit of a heady sensation. Not quite what I would call light-headedness but something that is affecting the feeling in my head.

(Long pause)

RON: It's almost as if what I feel as a veil between the medium and Bob and myself is a fine mist. I wouldn't call it mist but fine—I do not really know what to call it, but there is a fine energy between the medium and the two of us that almost looks a bit like a wall.

(Long pause. Carole Lynne comes out of the energy so that she can speak for a moment in her own voice.)

CAROLE LYNNE AGAIN IN HER OWN VOICE: I am able to speak too. I feel surrounded by a coating; I felt it wrapped around me. At one moment I felt a little bit scared because it was almost like being cocooned in something. And then I felt this energy that is wrapping around me go out to the two of you. And just after I felt that, you said (referring to Ron) that you saw this veil.

(Pause)

CAROLE LYNNE STILL IN HER OWN VOICE: This is a very different experience, unexpected. Actually, I am just going to sit with it and see. I am going to ask My Guidance what is going on.

(Long pause)

THE ENERGY: We have spoken to you about energy. We have spoken to you about strands of energy that move throughout the universe picking up knowledge and leaving off knowledge. We are showing you, in this moment, what it looks like. We are around you to feel what the energy feels like.

When you are giving a reading, a little bit of this energy surrounds you as it connects you, as if it were connecting energy. It connects you with the communicators that are coming in. In this moment you have more energy around you than you would be able to tolerate when doing a regular mediumistic reading, but in this state we are able to demonstrate to you more, the density of this energy. Not everyone has seen the energy, but a clairvoyant can see it quite clearly.

Can you see a shift, Ron?

RON: I do see a shift, and I notice an iridescence that I didn't notice before, very close to the face of the medium. I see around and above you almost a rose color. But I was not sure if that rose color was a reflection of the red light in the room or if it was something different. What I am seeing now is more of a white color, and I am feeling a less intense energy than I was feeling a moment ago. It seems lighter.

THE ENERGY: Bob, can you feel tingling?

BOB: No, I can't.

THE ENERGY: Sometimes when you are sleeping our energy is around you, and we are able to communicate with human beings much more easily. The energy is now very healing.

RON: I can't help but comment that just prior to the medium saying those words I felt healing energy come in.

(Now the conversation in the session stops, and the Energy leads what we human beings would call "a healing session"— sending healing energy to each member of the group. As this is happening, my perception is that we are cocooned within this mist that Ron has described at the beginning of the session—a mist that I was experiencing *before* Ron said anything about it. After the healing session is completed, the Energy resumes the conversation.)

THE ENERGY: What are your questions?

BOB: I can feel an overall quiet at this time, but I do not feel some of the other physical manifestations or the visual ones which Ron can feel and see.

THE ENERGY: That is because he is clairvoyant.

BOB: I understand. At the same time I keep feeling that it is because I am trying too hard, and that is somewhat of a paradox because I think the ability would be there regardless of how hard you try.

THE ENERGY: It has been agreed, right from the start, that it would be good for the project to have one clairvoyant and one who is not so that we can know what is going on.

BOB: Yes.

THE ENERGY: So for the project as a whole it is good.

BOB: Well, at some point I hope to be able to see some of this.

THE ENERGY: What questions do you have?

BOB: My main question is about the struggle I am having with focusing on the things of my life. Perhaps I am trying too hard when there might be a simple way to deal with it.

THE ENERGY: This thought that you have about yourself is like a groove in a record, and it is playing over and over and over. It is a belief that you have about yourself. As long as you believe that you are unable to change, that thought will be there, and that thought will manifest as such.

So the simplicity that you are looking for is simply changing your mind and deciding that you are not like that. There is a part of you that lives the way that you say you are, but there are other parts of you, and all you have to do is simply call on them and exercise those parts of yourself. Just wake up in the morning and begin differently.

BOB: Thank you, and I do have a feeling that there is an easier way. I am trying too hard and trying to think it through rather than just doing it.

THE ENERGY: It is not a matter of thought.

BOB: I understand.

THE ENERGY: It is a matter of just deciding to do things differently. It is the giving up of the image of yourself that you have and, in a sense, putting in another disc. Not talking about it, not analyzing it, just doing it. And if there are other recordings that play, just say, "I don't want that." And go on about whatever you are doing.

BOB: I understand and will try to do it. I get caught up in thinking, and I should be doing.

THE ENERGY: You are caught in your thoughts. This is a time to do and enjoy and let your soul express itself. There will be various health and health things in life that all human beings go through because they have bodies, but the spirit within you is free of all that.

BOB: Thank you. I would like to step onto a different path.

RON: The question that I have relates to my day-to-day activities. I am very caught up in the energy I feel coming through me. I feel there must be some utility in using that energy on a day-to-day basis. What recommendations do you have to help me use this energy in my daily activities?

THE ENERGY: Good question. The energy is there streaming throughout the universe. The energy that you feel flowing through the channel in a formalized way at the moment is there and everywhere at all times. This energy is interplanetary. It is not just of the earth. It is more universal, and so when there are times during the day when you feel fatigued, you have only to tune in to the frequency and bring in energy. This is a better boost than any sugar one can use. It can maintain the human body throughout the day and throughout the night. Human beings do not realize that they are not their physical bodies. They do not realize that the energy that is coming through them is cosmic and that their physical bodies are such a small part of the energy that they are.

There is a certain condensation of energy that happens to create a physical body that separates Ron from Bob from Carole: three different densities of energy. But all of our energies are flowing into each other, and ultimately the energy is flowing through all of you from the entire universe. And yet human beings will focus on the Coke machine for their energy, but that is not where they need to get it. It needs to come in through the etheric body, through the outer body, and then be channeled in to the physical realm and the mental realm and the spiritual realm. Meditation is not necessary. All that is necessary is a bit of relaxation for a moment to receive the energy that is there, and then go on about one's work. It does not have to make you feel heady. It does not have to make you feel dizzy. It can be very subtle. It is dense in this moment, as we need the channel to be in this density of energy for her to be able to hold the kind of energy that we are bringing through and to allow her to put words on the energy. Were she not delivering these words, she would not need the density that she is experiencing right now.

Does that at all address your question?

RON: It is very helpful to me, especially the latter part of the explanation. Without that explanation, I might have expected to have this same energy come close to me during my workday.

THE ENERGY: Not the kind of energy the channel is in at the moment, no. When you are in your workday, you would need to tune in to a much lighter energy.

RON: Thank you. I appreciate the explanation.

BOB: The channel had a question. She is interested in anything you might like to say to her regarding her challenge to lose weight.

THE ENERGY: All that we have been talking about applies. The energy that she needs is in the cosmos. She does not need as much food, but when she gets tired, she naturally reaches for food. Less food means less weight, and when she is able to get her energy elsewhere, her weight will go down. When she thinks of herself in a certain way, her thoughts get stuck in a groove. She is thinking of herself as a certain weight. She has to let go of that image and that thought; it is an old pattern. She needs to wake up one morning and simply not eat as much anymore. She does not need it.

BOB: Thank you.

THE ENERGY: We are experimenting tonight. The energy is very strong around the channel, but she can move her feet tonight, whereas before we would not allow her to move her feet. So she can feel her feet, and she can feel her mouth and her eyes somewhat. But we have a stronger energy, starting at about the chin, coming down below her knees. This is an experiment.

BOB: Is the channel able to express how she feels at this time?

THE ENERGY: No, she can hear what is going on, but she is to the side.

BOB: I understand.

THE ENERGY: We are using her mind to clothe the waves of energy with words.

(Long pause)

Healing is being sent to a dog. It is not your dog, but someone else's dog close to you, Ron. Do you understand about a dog that needs healing?

RON: Yes, I do.

THE ENERGY: Not your dog.

RON: Not my dog.

THE ENERGY: And Bob, can you avoid major transactions in the next ten days?

BOB: As in financial?

THE ENERGY: Yes.

BOB: I will certainly try to do that.

(Pause)

THE ENERGY: And Carole must stay calm and not blow things out of proportion. There are many spirits who want to come through on this evening. But it feels important to stay focused on understanding this energy. For the three of you this has far greater implications at this time than bringing through a particular spirit. We hope you are not disappointed.

RON: I am not disappointed in the least.

BOB: I am not disappointed. I see this as an opportunity, as you say, to learn more about the context within which we all exist.

THE ENERGY: Well put.

(Pause)

THE ENERGY: What other questions?

RON: In respect to the experimentation that this Energy is doing with the medium, is there a reason behind the experimentation? Is there something that the Energy feels that it will gain through this experimentation?

THE ENERGY: We would like to see if less of the physical body can be numb in order for the waves to be contained in the physical body. We have freed up various parts. We feel that the channel is getting used to being able to hold the waves of energy as they pass through, so we are experimenting with how numb she needs to be for this to happen.

BOB: I recently was with a group of people who were experiencing various demonstrations of interaction with spirit. It included one they call "trance," but it was a very different type of trance than I had observed previously in that the physical body of the medium that was being taken over by spirit was very active—in one case walking around very animatedly, very naturally, as a human body would normally do, and in another case sitting with the body position and facial expression changing quite readily as two different spirits came through. How would that be different from what our channel is experiencing this evening?

THE ENERGY: There is no relationship between the two. When the channel has brought through a particular entity, then it is more like what you have seen and just described. You have had sessions where there have been lost spirits or different entities coming through. But in this case, the channel is more like a radio—a radio antenna that is picking up waves of energy and translating this into words. We are not a person. As we have told you before, we do not even like to use words like *we* and ultimately we are wordless. We do not live anywhere. We are not seen in form. We are connection. We are creation.

The channel does her best to put words to it through her human mind, but falls short of a real explanation.

BOB: I think that is sufficient for the moment. I understand the difference.

THE ENERGY: Many mediums who are in trance are interpreting the energy of the spirit that lived. More of them (the spirits) actually dramatizing themselves. Because the spirits are in a different form. They do not behave the same way anymore. The medium perceives them in human form and demonstrates them in human form. And as the medium picks up on the energy and the memories of that human form that once lived, those are then played out through the medium like a video, like a drama. But it is coming through the personality of the medium. That does not make it less authentic.

BOB: I understand that there is a difference, and I appreciate that. I am interested in your comment that the trance medium is, in fact, interpreting, as you say, spirit as spirit. So my sense is that the medium is trying to understand what that spirit was like in order to relate it to us, translate to us, because that is our only reference.

THE ENERGY: Right. No such thing as a pure transmission of spirit.

BOB: I understand.

THE ENERGY: The channel speaking today—it is coming through her. Every human being who has ever had a revelation, that revelation has come through the mind, spiritual body, etheric body, of that individual consciousness. We are wordless. So anything that has words is already an approximation. There is no way to reproduce us authentically. When a medium does a reading, which you would call a regular reading, the medium is receiving the energy of the spirit and must then relate it in words. But the spirit is no longer speaking in words.

BOB: I understand, and I have learned something.

THE ENERGY: Not everyone would agree with it. Even with direct voice, it is not as direct as one would assume. The energy of the spirit is there, but it must be translated back into human terms again. The spirit is not human in the same sense anymore.

If the three of you sitting here were to suddenly have your physical bodies removed, you would be pure spirit. It is your physical body, your mental body, and your emotional body that allow you to speak in the way that you do, because that is part of your human condition. So as mediums, in whatever form you are involved in, you are expressing it in your own human terms. Again, that does not mean that a communication is not happening.

BOB: I had not thought of it in that way before. That is fascinating.

THE ENERGY: There is no way to divorce the mind, body, and spirit of the medium from the communication that happens in any form of spirit communication.

Everything is a translation. What you are hearing now is a translation. Were this same burst of energy to be sent to a different channel, the words and the thoughts would be slightly different.

BOB: Again, much like our radio which has a receiver tuned to a particular frequency, and if it is the right frequency, the communication will come through in a way that you can understand. If it is slightly different, then all we get is static that is not translated properly. So the connection, the translation, is important. I would say the effectiveness of the medium in that translation process is a factor of the medium's practice and ability to do that and the ability to raise their frequency level as needed.

THE ENERGY: We are almost ready for some sessions with no words. Not today, not soon. As the three of you sit, you are learning to hold this energy. You are absorbing it. It is affecting you. You have only to think back a couple of years, and all of you will note that you have changed in some way.

BOB: We appreciate the opportunity to learn in this way.

THE ENERGY: Just for a moment, let us be without words.

(Pause)

(The tape ends, and there is a lot of noise as one of the sitters turns the tape over. Carole Lynne is jolted by the sudden noise and begins to cough.)

THE ENERGY: You will receive so much more without words, without thinking.

(The channel begins to cough.)

THE ENERGY: It is time to bring the channel out.

(Carole Lynne continues to cough.)

THE ENERGY: We ask Ron to count from one to ten.

(Carole Lynne still coughs and chokes a bit. The session ends prematurely, but Carole needs to come back to a normal state of consciousness.)

Comments

It was a shame that this session had to end so abruptly, but this is what can happen when a medium is entranced and there is a sudden noise. After this experience, we no longer used tapes that would need to be turned over. To an entranced medium, the sound of changing a cassette tape can feel like the noise of an airplane right next to the medium's ear.

One of the most important things that happened in this session was my experience of a mist forming around me and then around all of us, and Ron mentioning this mist without my having said anything about it. For me, Ron's comments confirmed what I was experiencing.

It was exciting for all of us to experience spirit in a new way. Up until this session, the sitters had heard words come through me and had seen energies that overshadowed me, but this was the first time a mist was seen around us. And it was the first time that we were told that someday we would have sessions where we would communicate without words.

Ron was very excited about seeing the mist. He said he had seen a shimmery kind of veil in front of me. I replied that it was like having gossamer all around me. It was very ethereal, and I could see it clairvoyantly. Ron then shared that when he saw this mist, he began to feel light-headed. I shared that I had first seen this mist form around me, and then I saw it form around Ron and Bob as well.

Ron commented, "I kept really having problems with what I was seeing as shifting in your body. That almost reminded me of a Picasso painting, the way it was, because it was cubism—like this section of your body seemed to be compressed and then your arm seemed shorter and your head just seemed different to me."

Bob said he noticed I was able to move my feet during the session, and he had not seen me do that in previous sessions. He felt that somehow the Energy helped me to loosen up parts of my body.

Ron said I must have felt cocooned, and I replied that I felt like I was a moth. He said it was as if I were in a chrysalis, but a mist that was not as dense as a chrysalis.

I said that I had gotten scared, and there was a moment that I felt very claustrophobic. I felt the mist coming in on me and wondered when it was going to stop. I was not happy at all, and I was considering coming out of the energy. But I managed to control myself, and the mist did not come any farther toward me.

Bob said, "Well, your face did look a little screwed-up, almost as if you were trying to resist. You were tightening up, and then it gradually became a pensive look."

"Well, I do have control," I said. "I can come out at any time that I need to. I can talk to the Energy and say 'I need out,' which I did when that thing (the sound of the tape being changed) went off. Learning to trust that I am in control was what my whole first two years of channeling were about. I needed to learn that I could come out when I wanted to. Now I feel like I am in a different phase here. Tonight I felt like I graduated into something new: I could take in and sustain the energy. It is not that I am any smarter or wiser. It has to do with the fact that now my body can take it. It has taken since 1987 for my body to be able to sustain whatever that was that was wrapped around me. Even though I was a little scared, I was able to stay in the energy when this mist wrapped around us."

"Is it that you have some greater level of trust in the relationship with the energy, so in a sense you are relaxing a little bit more?" Bob asked.

"It doesn't feel like that to me," I said. "All along it has felt to me as if I have been rewired. These channeling experiences are totally changing my mediumship. It terrifies me, as it is like a whole other world. When I give private readings now, I am in such a deep state. I mean, I am talking to the people in spirit, and if I do not come out of that trance state carefully, I could fall right over. I could never allow myself to go into such a deep state when doing mediumship in platform demonstrations."

"Unless you were in controlled conditions, and you were trying to do that," Bob noted.

"I do not know what is going to happen," I said.

All three of us laughed about the possibility of my doing trance work on the platform, then I said, "I know that in the private readings I am in a deeper state and the spirits are coming through very differently. It is very clear to me now that spirit is vibration, at least in the way that I am receiving it. I received it in a different way years ago because that is how I needed to receive the spirit at that time."

"Yes," Ron said. "It is the difference between experiencing spirit as a vibration and talking about the theory that spirit is a vibration."

"Right, yes," I agreed. "I am seeing what somebody in spirit used to look like physically. And that is probably one of my stronger points in a reading: knowing what the color of their hair was and all that. But it is very clear to me that the spirits are not like that . . . It is like this: the energy manifests itself for a minute so that I can *see*. And that is perhaps what spirit did in physical mediumship when the ectoplasm would come out. What was around me felt like it was a much finer kind of a thing, but along those same lines—not ectoplasm but a variety of it.

"Now, when I am giving a reading, after the spirit has manifested itself within my mind to show me how he or she looked when alive, then that vision is gone for the rest of the reading, and I am experiencing the spirit as energy.

"So I have felt that I have been rewired so that I am able to pick up on the energy and vibration of those in spirit."

"That makes sense to me," Ron said. "As what happens with the body as it begins to grow? It grows nerves, and we know that nerves can regenerate when they have been damaged over a course of time."

"Now where is our work going?" I asked. "I don't know, but I feel like something different is beginning to happen. I feel like it is going to be important to observe what can be seen in our energy fields."

"I know the Energy says that we are not going to have a wordless session soon, but we're moving a bit in that direction," Ron said. "And that is . . . very interesting. I am sure that you will find that very intriguing once it happens."

"We'll have to work on our telepathy," Bob said. "I hope I won't be speechless!"

The Sitting Project

At Bob's comment, we ended the session in laughter.

As you understand by now, I am aware of what is going on even when I am in a very deep state. In this state I usually feel totally numb except for my mouth and tongue. And it feels to me like the part of me that is my observing mind or self sits up on the left-hand side of my head until it is time to come back into my physical body as the session is concluding.

In the August 13, 2007, session, the Energy decided to experiment with me. I was able to feel my feet, which I found wonderful, as it is always so difficult to come out of a trance session with my feet feeling frozen and numb. I can fully appreciate that, even now, I need to be in quite a deep state as the energy pours through me. I do not think I could "hold" the energy in a normal state of consciousness. But someday I hope that I can feel slightly sleepy instead of having to feel like most of my body is frozen. Quite frankly, I hope that ultimately I can go into a much lighter state when I am bringing through knowledge from My Guidance.

When I first learned about trance mediumship, I heard that the deeper the state of trance, the more authentic the delivered message would be, because there is more assurance that the medium will not interfere by adding his or her own thoughts to what is coming through. When I have done channeling sessions, I have been in a deep state, but there has always been a part of me that is aware of what is going on. I always felt guilty about that, and I wondered if I was not measuring up. Most people whom I confided in used to assure me that one day I would fall into a deeper state and no longer be conscious of what was going on. They spoke of this deeper state as something I should work toward achieving.

I thanked them politely. Intuitively, I did not feel that my work would develop in the same mode and that I would always be aware of what was happening. At least I hoped and prayed I would. Why would I want to miss the whole experience when I could be learning so much?

As of 2008, I am hearing that more mediums believe trance work is changing and some mediums are beginning to be more aware of what is happening while they are in trance than they had been in the past. Quite frankly, I am grateful to be part of a generation of trance mediums that do not all feel that they have to go to sleep. Perhaps I am part of a new wave of trance work in which the spirit world is working differently than it used to.

Recently, I heard a story about a student taking a class in trance mediumship, and this student, like most students who take trance workshops, was still under the impression that the deeper the trance state the higher the mark one gets from the teacher. On this particular day, this student went into trance. A lot of conversation took place between the supposedly entranced medium and other members of the class. When the student medium came out of trance, the teacher asked her, "So what happened during the session?" The student replied, "Oh, I do not know, as I was totally out. I do not remember anything." The teacher did not think the student had been totally unaware of what was going on and felt that the student just said she was without any recall in order to make a good impression. She replied to the student, "Well, it is good you were totally out because absolutely nothing happened. We all sat here quietly the whole time." The student's eyes were wide, and her mouth dropped open in surprise. But, of course, she could not refute the teacher's claim, as she has been supposedly "totally out."

As I relate this story to you, I am happier than ever that, during all my early years of trance work, I never knew that what I was doing was called trance. I had bought a book on channeling, and I was experimenting on my own with the help of what I called my "channeling facilitator": Moriah Marston, a well-known channel. While she did not sit in on any of my channeling sessions, I did meet with her a couple times a month for two years to tell her what was going on. Her only job was to make sure I did not get into any psychological trouble. But she never told me how to channel because I asked her to allow me to let spirit guide me. I was free to experience and develop as a trance medium without a lot of people telling me how to do it and what to aim for.

Perhaps if I had been in a channeling or trance class, I would have learned to look for a spirit guide who would appear to me in a purple cape. Left to my own devices, I experienced the Energy, which came to me at first as a loving presence and spoke to me in many riddles and rhymes, and that later, in the Sitting Project, showed us that what I had always called My Guidance was not the spirit of a person who had lived on earth, but an energy that was creative knowledge.

November 12, 2007: This Energy Is Moving

"By the time someone has understood it, it will have changed and moved on because it is evolution. Perhaps it is something so simple that humanity complicates. In its simple form, it is incredible healing."

In attendance:

Channel: Carole Lynne
Sitter: Ron Monroe
Sitter: Bob Blake
Guest: Rev. Simeon Stefanidakis

Meet Rev. Simeon Stefanidakis

Reverend Simeon Stefanidakis, from the First Spiritual Temple in Brookline, Massachusetts, is a highly respected church pastor, teacher, and medium who is invited to lecture and do demonstrations of mediumship in the United States and England. As an author, he has written many courses for the First Spiritual Temple, as well as having written the content for the temple's website, *www.fst.org*—the best website on Spiritualism that I have ever seen to date.

I felt that Rev. Simeon would add a great deal to the Sitting Project, as he has had years of experience working with Rev. Stephen Fulton, a pastor of the temple, who has been a trance medium for over thirty years. In my opinion, those who sit for and work with trance mediums can often know more about trance mediumship than those who are in trance, as many in trance have no recall of what occurs during a trance session or have only partial recall, as I do.

I had met Rev. Simeon many years earlier, and we had become good friends. During the past three years, we had discussed our experiences with mediumship and our work as ministers. Ron and Bob had met and studied with both Brenda Lawrence and Nora Shaw, our previous guests, but neither one of them had ever worked with Rev. Simeon.

CAROLE LYNNE STILL IN HER OWN VOICE: I feel spirit around me.

RON: Does the channel need some help in being counted down?

(I nod. Ron counts slowing from ten to one as I go into an altered state of consciousness.)

THE ENERGY: The past few times we have met, there has been much discussion about what you have come to call the Energy (and) the channel calls her Guidance. We have told you that you cannot personify us because we are not human; we are not in any form that you can conceive of. We are spheres of light, which contain the knowledge of the universe.

Tonight we are showing the channel a personification of us because that is what human beings do in order to try to understand us.

You must know that there is the image of a woman superimposed over her, and, were she not to have the knowledge that we are not personified, she would think that she is seeing and feeling the presence of a female spirit. But it is an image that is going through her mind because it helps her to see who we are, and this is how most human beings perceive of their spirit guides.

This is how human beings in ancient times perceived of the gods, but it is all energy. Not that there are not some guides who are human beings who have walked this earth and not that you do not have loved ones who come through to speak to you. But the greater percentage of guidance that does come through is not personified. It is human beings who personify this energy so that they can understand it.

There is a loving hand of a female guide. There is a great brightness you see in this moment.

You may speak now.

RON: I am very much aware of an energy that feels quite nurturing. It seems associated with the guidance and the words that are coming through. Is there a particular reason for that nurturing feeling coming through now?

THE ENERGY: There is no particular reason. It is to demonstrate to you how you human beings respond to us. The word *us* cannot be used, as has been said before. It is used for convenience.

There is no spirit of a woman here. There is the energy—the nurturing energy that you are perceiving—and we are allowing it within the channel to be perceived as the image of a woman. Do you understand?

RON: Yes, I understand.

SIMEON: I am reminded of what one medium said many years ago that very often the guides do need to assume a persona in order to satisfy the human condition. So I understand what you are saying.

My question would be about you, or the essence of you. From what I understand you are one who has not come to this earth before incarnate. Do you have any connection with the earthly condition? Have you focused in another realm—another realm of spirit?

THE ENERGY: The essence that is coming through the channel is (the) vibration of knowledge. The word(s) *we, you,* or *your* cannot be applied. Truth is light, and light throughout the universe has the knowledge, has the expression, of creation of all that is.

The energy that we are, if we must use the word *we,* is the same as you. This energy moves throughout cosmic reality learning and bringing information from one source to another. This energy picks up information and drops it off. Then energy is creative force. There are no words really to describe it. But the channel receives waves of this vibration and, when in a higher state of consciousness, can put words to it. In her normal state of consciousness, these words would not come the same way.

It is understandable that one is disoriented, receiving this kind of message. We are connection. We are impulse. We are vital force. We don't come from any planet or realm.

All that is creativity comes from this energy. But human beings, as they receive this energy through the higher self, give expression to it in many, many different ways: in science, in art, in music, and in imagination of spirit guides.

You may speak.

SIMEON: I hear what you are saying and very definitely it makes sense to me. My question would be, again, what is the intent, if I may ask, in working with this particular instrument? Do you have a specific goal as your spirit or your essence blends with her intelligence or mind?

(When Simeon uses the word *instrument,* he is referring to the channel, Carole Lynne.)

THE ENERGY: That is a good question. I ask for a moment.

The most important reason we work with anyone is the healing. There is a part of each soul that links with this creative force, and to know this creative force is to heal. This particular channel was able to receive us easily because of her creativity. And in the early years of channeling, many stories and poems and rhymes came through that were obviously not anything she would write, when compared to her own work. And it is not that we wrote it either. It is that as the energy came through the instrument in a higher state of consciousness; the higher state of consciousness interpreted the energy from the perspective that the conscious Carole could not. Do you understand?

SIMEON: I do.

THE ENERGY: It took many years of work before she was able to bring through the energy that is now coming through. All the early years were very different. She would be nauseous; she would almost pass out from the energy coming through her. Now we are beginning to reach a time when she will actually be able to feel more of her physical body, because it will not destruct her. Right now she can only feel her mouth.

We do not have a particular goal with Carole. She has been willing to receive us. And any mind, any higher consciousness state that any human being can open up, will then receive this energy, as it is of a higher state of consciousness. This energy does not belong to this channel. She is tuned into the frequency of it and is able to interpret it when in a deeper state. If you were to go into that state, you would express it differently. There might be similar strands of expression, but it would be different. And you would find that if you express thoughts in your everyday consciousness, it would be quite different than when going into this state.

You may speak.

SIMEON: I have a thousand questions to ask, but I understand what you are saying. I am intrigued by one thing you do say, that—

and this will lead to a question actually—but I am intrigued by your comment that Carole has to interpret the essence of this truth, this wisdom that is there. Number one, would I be correct in saying that one difference between now and the past is that she, herself, is spiritually more fine-tuned, so to speak, so that she can be a more clear instrument for this wisdom? And number two, in her interpreting this, is not her own mind/consciousness perhaps interfering?

THE ENERGY: All mediumship is interpretation.

When the grandmother spirit comes to you for one of your clients, from the perspective of what is being said, it is an energy, a wave of energy that you tune in to. And while you may say, "Grandmother is saying this and that," Grandmother's energy is blending with yours, and it is your Higher Self that is able to tune into that energy and, in a sense, decode it and know what Grandmother means. But Grandmother doesn't talk anymore in that same way. I know it is not accepted everywhere, but the statement being made is that ultimately all spirit communication is blended energy and has to go through the mind of the medium.

Direct voice is not even always what it seems to be. It is a projection of how the spirit used to sound, and even mental mediumship is a projection of how the spirit used to look. Have you not noticed that sometimes spirits show themselves in different ways at different ages?

And the spirits are not all as separated, as mediums seem to think.

As these words come through the channel, she does not always agree with what is being said now. But it has to be said that the energy of spirits is blending, and when a family unit comes in, they come in as a blended energy. Just as human beings would like to personify guides, human beings would like to personify and organize spirit communication in a way that is not real. That does not make it any less authentic, but the medium must tune in to the frequency and decode it. It is the energy that is the spirit. It is that unique consciousness of a spirit that is there, that the medium is able to tune in to, and then the medium must speak it.

If you were in the land of frogs, the frogs would interpret it. Do you understand?

Put your mind to the side for the moment and consider it. So, yes, the energy is interpreted through the higher consciousness of the medium, and if this same energy would be picked up in this moment by Ron, Ron might say similar things but put it into different words, because we are not words anyway. There are no direct words. We are a whole other realm, and it cannot be said that we are "we." This explanation is an attempt of the higher consciousness of a mind to put form and words to something that is formless and wordless. This is what human beings have done throughout all of human history. This is where all the religions, all your gods, all your poetry, all your science comes from.

You may speak.

SIMEON: I am absolutely intrigued with what you are saying. Correct me if I am wrong. Are you saying that in spirit there is not the degree of separateness of identity as perhaps we think there is, and therefore, when we link with a specific loved one, very often other influences can come into play there, because there isn't that distinction that we may so strongly believe in? Am I correct in that?

THE ENERGY: Yes.

SIMEON: That answers a lot of questions. Thank you. I appreciate that.

RON: In light of that same question, it seems we work very hard to personify those projections. Should we instead be trying to sort out how to blend with the spirit? By blending, wouldn't we then know how the spirit connects with different family members and even with others in spirit?

THE ENERGY: It is not the issue of many. Before going into that kind of question, one needs to understand how spirit communicates. Mediums have made spirit communication something it is not. The spirit is there—and the instrument wants to fight with me at this moment—the instrument is there, the spirit is there. But a great deal of the nuances that the medium picks up, the medium is picking up from the client. The spirit is there, but in a different way than is portrayed. Just as people must portray spirit guides and give them long histories, people portray their loved ones as if they were next door. There is no real sense of them being in the spirit world. "Look, I've got your grandmother here, and she says blah blah blah. She says this, and she says that." Well, it depends on what level the soul of grandmother is in at the moment. Very few true communications happen. It is useful, what happens between mediums and clients, because people living on earth want to hear from their loved ones in spirit, and the energy of the medium is there. And the medium does tune in to that energy, but the whole way that the spirit is described and animated, as if a person living and walking and talking, is for the convenience of the medium and the relatives still living. It is not a very true portrayal of spiritual life.

A truer portrayal would not be understood by most people. That is why it is given in the way that it is done now. Clients would not hear what they want to hear. A truer portrayal, the evolution of the soul of that particular spirit, where they are in their evolution—people would not want to hear it. It would be confusing.

You may speak.

BOB: It occurs to me that you are an energy field. It seems pertinent to this definition. One of the main purposes of mediumship and the sense of energy making itself available through a channel is for the purpose of healing—to come to a common understanding between the energy and the person who is receiving the message, with the help of the channel. To provide that personification that would, in fact, cause healing or promote healing for the listener.

THE ENERGY: The personification is very helpful for human beings. But this channel is seeing the reality above and behind the personification, which is projected. Do you understand?

BOB: I do understand. I believe that the best way I can understand that is that there is a higher resonance with the channel than I have, which enables her to see what you are offering and I cannot. At least I am aware of it.

THE ENERGY: You can, but it is not your choice. It has been said before that this energy does not belong to this instrument; we are not her guide, her possession.

BOB: I understand that, and my sense is that she has proved her abilities to be aware of your energy more than I have.

THE ENERGY: It is a practice since 1987, with some years off in between.

SIMEON: May I ask a question? It sounds to me that what you are saying is that what is being channeled, or whatever term you wish to put on it, is just—well not just—but is a presence of truth, knowledge, insight that is just here throughout the whole of creation, as opposed to a specific individual or group of individuals. Is that a correct understanding?

THE ENERGY: Yes.

SIMEON: And I have always believed that as we evolve in spirit, that "we"—our individuality—expands, and what we perceive as me, a few years down the road, will be much expanded from what I may perceive as me today. It sounds also to me that you're saying that mediumship should endeavor to focus more on the spirit of the spirit, as opposed to the personalities of spirit. Is that correct?

THE ENERGY: To begin, we are not saying anything. The channel is reading what is there. It is energy that is there, and it is as if the antenna is picking up the frequency and interpreting what is there. We are not saying how mediumship should be done. It is none of our business.

The truth is that spirit on a higher level is different than the projections that most mediums receive. That does not mean that mediumship is not authentic, but there are very different levels of translation, because all mediumship is translation and decoding of energy. There are different levels of translation and projection.

Perhaps one needs to put value when we say different mediums have different jobs, but even that is just for convenience; that is not a correct interpretation. That is the channel's inner feeling at the moment, trying to make sense of what she doesn't want to hear.

SIMEON: So this is working basically as (if) the channel is reading something.

THE ENERGY: *Reading* is the closest word we can use—perceiving.

SIMEON: A natural question would be, where did that come from? Who put that there? How did that originate? If there is something to be read, then someone, some group of beings had to, I want to say, inscribe it in that essence. Is that a collective inscription from the whole of creation?

It sounds almost like she is talking almost to the Akasha.

(Rev. Simeon defines the Akashic Records to be a mental and energy recording and reflection of every soul in Creation.)

THE ENERGY: Creation has evolved and continues to evolve. And there is more and more knowledge, and there is more and more truth. It is not like a record of everything that has happened or will happen. It is not like that. Some have written that the world and the universe is the mind of the Creator. Those words may come close to it. Human beings have given it many different labels and names: this energy, this knowledge, this truth.

And human beings will continue to perceive it differently because the antenna of each one who perceives it is different, depending on the soul of that individual. There is an interaction of the truth and the knowledge and the soul of each individual, which is a part of that whole.

There are more names than anyone could ever remember. But again, that is the struggle: to somehow take this knowledge, this truth, and put it in a box, capture it, label it, understand it, prove it. This energy is moving, and it is vital, and it is creative, and it will never be put in anything.

By the time someone has understood it, it will have changed and moved on because it is evolution. Perhaps it is something so simple that humanity complicates. In its simple form, it is incredible healing.

RON: From a physical standpoint, I find it difficult to understand some of the information. This is because of my orientation. I try to understand from a physical perspective. As I become more aware of what I am seeing without eyes, hearing without ears, my mind is expanded. As a result, it feels as though I change my rate of vibration. When I succeed, I am better able to understand. Is that fair to say?

THE ENERGY: In the world of spirit are vibration. As you blend with the soul that no longer has a physical body, projections will come to you to help you understand the life of that person on earth. They are projections that you interpret. There will come a point that these projections will no longer be necessary because you will simply know; it will come to you as a knowing.

Understanding really that spirit is vibration is important for healing, because when spirit is seen as something to gather information from, the energetic transfer is . . . (words missing here), and there is a real blending between the energy of the spirit and the energy of the medium. This has been translated as very powerful energy, but the loved ones still living can feel it.

Do you understand?

RON: Yes.

SIMEON: May I ask, in what you are offering us, how does the presence of evil, on this earthly condition, come into play here?

Within a world that is not all a reflection of someone, from what you are saying, I surmise that to some degree there is also included in the state of spirit the presence of evil.

THE ENERGY: Evolution has many stories to tell, and not all souls are highly evolved. In the world of spirit, there will be those who are highly evolved and those who are not, just as on the earth plane or in many other realms of life.

Is that what you are getting at?

SIMEON: I am not really getting at anything. I was just more interested in this state of spirit that you speak of, which I firmly believe is there, here, in this condition.

THE ENERGY: If you are speaking of a medium connecting with a spirit at the level that the spirit is in terms of their spirit evolution . . . So if there is a spirit that is not evolved, there may be negative energy.

RON: For the sake of the channel, it is important to mention that we are coming to nearly the end of an hour of conversation. We have about seven minutes.

THE ENERGY: Sometimes human beings have talked about evil as being separation from God. This instrument does not perceive the negative energies as evil, but as needing great help.

SIMEON: It is a word that unfortunately we communicate, using the language that we have.

THE ENERGY: It is the choice of the society. What do you really want to say about evil?

SIMEON: Well, personally, I have always felt—and I am not sure if I just interpreted what you just said correctly—but I have always felt that if God is all, then evil must be part of God as well. And we can't take one part of creation and separate it from the whole. And this is a very perplexing question. I try to pose this to people, and it is a very difficult concept for people to understand or to even want to understand. But evil is a shadowing of the light of divinity within.

THE ENERGY: As human beings evolve and are less negative, the whole spiritual evolution will become more positive. There is a way that Divine Consciousness is affected by the decisions of living forms.

What some would call evil are in ignorance, because there is a creation that is negative, by your words and your feeling. Every human being has negative—or, if you like, evil—impulses within. It is how each human being decides to progress.

We would like to go on, but this is a long time for the channel. Thank you very much.

RON: If the channel is ready, we will begin counting.

(Ron counts slowly from one to ten as I come out of the trance state.)

Comments

"We are connection. We are impulse. We are vital force." These words inspired me as I read the transcription. It is exciting to perceive of an energy that is the core of all that is creative and is perhaps part of the energy that created the universes and that still creates all that exists. And the idea that creative people, as well as scientists, are inspired by spirit is not a new thought for any of us. We have all heard stories about creative artists or scientists who receive their most important inspirations through dreams.

But it was extremely disconcerting for all of us attending the session to hear that sometimes when we feel we are communicating with individual guides, we are actually creating their images with our imagination. Those of us in the room were faced with a deep fear that we had had for many years: "Are we imagining our guides?"

It has been much easier for us to have confidence that our loved ones in spirit are communicating with us, as we have all received readings from mediums who have brought us information about our loved ones that they could not possibly have known. But proof that our spirit guides exist is not accessible in the same way; when a medium tells us we have a Chinese man for a guide, there is no way to prove that. If we ourselves have experienced a Chinese guide for many years, then perhaps the medium who mentions this guide is confirming our experience. But when a medium tells us about a guide we have not perceived, there is absolutely no way to prove the existence of that guide.

But in this session we heard words insinuating that we sometimes imagine our guides. This is an insult to many people who have deep beliefs about who their spirit guides are, what they look like, and where they come from. To hear words that imply that some of us, some of the time, may imagine our spirit guides, not only rocked our boats, but dumped us into the water gasping for air.

But let's look at what has been demonstrated to us in this session when the spirit of the lady appeared—the lady I felt superimposed over me and whom Ron felt as a very healing energy. This example may teach us something important.

For a moment, allow yourself to perceive that there are energies that are so spiritual and so connected to the Divine that they simply *have no human form*. Would we be able to perceive these energies in their original state? In my opinion, people of advanced spiritual evolution would be able to, but most human beings would not be able to perceive or receive these energies unless they were sent in the form the humans could understand: the form of an angel, a spirit guide, or another form that the human mind can relate to.

Let us say that Mary Smith is receiving guidance from the Divine. Mary uses the word *God,* as she was raised in a religion that uses that name. As Mary communicates with God, God sends his love in the form of an angel. The angel is not flesh and blood as Mary is. The angel Mary perceives is an image that

Mary experiences. This angel *is* a messenger from God. The fact that Mary perceives this energetic messenger as an angel, and another person, David Jones (who uses the name *Infinite Spirit* for the Divine), perceives an energetic messenger from the Infinite Spirit as a spirit guide, does not take away from the fact that "the God of their understanding" is talking to both of them. They are simply receiving the message and the messenger in different forms. They are both receiving love and guidance from the most Divine Consciousness, but they are receiving this love in different forms.

From my perspective, there is a source of all creation, and each one of us is a spark of that Divine Source. The Greater Self of each individual is able to communicate with Divine Source. Depending on our cultural background and life experience, we receive that communication in different ways. The communication from the Divine Source comes to us in waves of energy, which we then, each individually, decode and translate into a form that we can understand. This in *no* way takes away from the divinity or sacredness of the different images in which we receive the Divine Source. In fact, it makes the communication even more sacred as we realize that the Divine Source is ultimately beyond words, beyond images, and that is why many of us have to receive the communication in images we can comprehend.

But what about guides who seem to be the spirits of those who have once lived on the earth? Perhaps those guides, whose consciousness has survived death (just as your Uncle John's consciousness has survived death), do appear to you as they were when they once lived on the earth. So it is possible that the guide my friend Linda sees as a Native American chief really did live on the earth as a Native American chief, and now, in spiritual form, the guide presents himself to her in an image of the way he used to look when he was alive.

And perhaps there are some guides who never lived a life on earth, but who appear to us sometimes in the image of a human being so that we can perceive them. I use the word *perhaps* because there is no way to prove if my thoughts about spirit guides are true. And I am not going to insult your intelligence by looking up quotes from ten different spiritual texts and throwing them at you to prove my points. (Any savvy spiritual seeker knows that because most great spiritual texts say so many things, no matter what one is trying to prove, one can find a good quote that, when used out of context, can prove one's own point. To me this is pure nonsense.)

What I can offer you are my thoughts about spiritual guidance and guides, based on my personal experiences as I communicate with what I believe to be a power greater than myself— a Divine Source of Energy. And my opinion at the writing of this book is that when we communicate with guides that once lived on the earth, we may be seeing visions of how they used to look when they were alive. However, when we communicate with energies that are more cosmic and universal, our Greater-Selves are able to connect with these energies at the level of our own spiritual consciousness. At one level of spiritual development, we are presented with these energies in forms we can understand. As we continue on in spiritual development, we reach a level within our development where we can perceive of these energies without the need of a form, such as a guide who lived on earth, an angel, or other spiritual vision.

While I offer you my thoughts, I will not be imprisoned by any of my understandings for the rest of my life. In other words, I will not present my thoughts to you as the ultimate truth just for the sake of sounding more like an authority. As I continue to learn, my thoughts will change. I am not interested in trying to convert you to my way of thinking. I offer my experience in the hopes that it stimulates thoughts about your own experiences or provokes you to be open to having more connection with Divine Energy.

As a medium, I have had many questions about how the world of spirit is actually communicating with me. The messages in the November 12 session give us a lot of perspective on the ways that the spirit world has to project images that we, as human beings, can understand. What I understand from the messages in this session is that as we evolve in the world of spirit, we are in a different, more spiritual form than we are when on the earth. Spirits have to project images of what they used to be like.

I am also very affected by the messages about how the world of spirit is evolving just as we are. We are told that we are wasting our time trying to understand, label, and organize wisdom in such a way that we can put it into a box. By the time we think we understand, this creative force will have moved on.

Perhaps there is great truth in the concept that eternal wisdom is light and is beyond words. We cannot understand the truth through the words, labels, and categories we try to place "truth" in. Perhaps we receive the highest spiritual teachings when we can go beyond the mind, beyond words, and simply allow ourselves to merge with Divine Consciousness. In those moments there is a knowing.

Chapter 9

Reflections on the Sitting Project

~~~~~~~~~~~~~~~~~~~~~~~~~~~~

THE EXPERIENCES OF THE SITTING PROJECT and the transcripts of the sessions have given me a lot to ponder. The following are comments from one of our guests, as well as the two regular sitters. First, Rev. Simeon Stefanidakis sent a letter he titled "Thoughts on Session with Rev. Carole Lynne, Channel."

> When I was first invited to attend the channeling session with Rev. Carole Lynne, I jumped at the opportunity, because I have a very keen interest in trance mediumship and channeling. I have always felt that the dynamics, as well as the energy and mind associations which are exhibited in trance mediumship speak volumes about how mediumship, in general, works. I also feel that many aspects of awareness and the extent of the soul's consciousness can be addressed through an examination of trance mediumship.
>
> When the session began, I immediately felt intense love and, for lack of a better word, the "sacredness" of the experience about to unfold. There was a healing presence and a sense of Spirit which one rarely experiences in current-day mediumship. Although I was a bit unfamiliar with the manner in which Rev. Lynne achieved

the trance link with Spirit, and although it was her own voice which emanated from the body of Rev. Lynne, I knew, without a question, that some presence, energy, soul, consciousness—I still cannot define it accurately—was addressing us.

And this is what, in my opinion, made this session so remarkably unique. Over the years, I have had the privilege of working and sharing with many trance mediums. Without exception, the focus of communication has been part content and part personality, in varying degrees of proportion. In sitting with Rev. Lynne, I was immediately impressed by the fact that the source of the communication extended beyond a specific Spirit personality, or even *persona*. It was as if the consciousness of the medium was connected to a cosmic or universal source of information and insight, and this is what was being communicated to us. I am not even sure whether another Spirit entity was working here (I, personally, was unaware of any), or whether the medium, herself, was directly connected to this source of information and this is what was being channeled from her "higher" self and/or consciousness.

In many ways, it reminded me of the mediumship of Edgar Cayce. In the early stages of Edgar Cayce's work, it was suggested that he, himself, was in contact with the aforementioned source and this is what was being channeled; thus, he was once called "the Sleeping Prophet" and not a medium.

Was Rev. Lynne, like Edgar Cayce, "reading" the Akasha, the great storehouse of Creation's experiential journey, and passing this on to us? Was there a specific Spirit entity working with Rev. Lynne who simply did not wish to have any form of personality brought forth? The "communicator" took great lengths to suggest there was no specific individual involved in the communication, not even the medium. This, I must admit, still causes me to reflect on the nature of the experience. Perhaps—and I tend to feel this is the case—*mediumship* is not the correct term to define what actually took place on that evening.

Beyond this, what also piqued my interest was the information given to us concerning the role of the medium and how Spirit communication often takes place. There was an obvious attempt to redefine, or, at least, to expand, our perception and understanding of mediumship and what it is that actually occurs when Spirit comes forth for communication, either of an evidential or inspirational nature. This, alone, could distress many mediums, or, at least, cause them to rethink their involvement with Spirit.

Finally, the evening evolved into discussions which extended beyond mediumship. I must admit, this was the most enjoyable part of the evening for me. I could feel the "frustration" of the communicator trying to explain concepts which extend beyond, yet are intimately involved with, the earthly condition in words which are based upon earthly experience. This makes perfect sense to me. As a working medium, how often am I at a loss to express, in our language, what Spirit is sharing with me on a level which goes beyond language. It can be frustrating.

Like any information which passes through the lips of a human instrument, I did not accept everything which was spoken that evening without deep thought and personal reflection. Regardless of the source or the degree of direct contact with this source, the information which we heard had to pass through the consciousness of Rev.

Lynne's own soul. This, out of necessity, creates some degree of filtering and influence. Having said this, I feel such influence was minimal, and the information which I heard helped, in many ways, shed light on questions which I have been asking myself, from my own experiences as a medium.

I left the evening not quite sure of the mechanics of what I had just experienced; but this I know: dialogue with (not just from) Spirit took place, and, within that exchange of ideas, there was both *communication* and *communion*.

Ron Monroe's comments:

When we first began the project, I already had the sense that it would be very interesting and rewarding. . . . I feel that over the course of the first several meetings I was able to begin to sense energy better. As we worked with spirits that came closer, I felt the presence. It didn't matter if the details were right or wrong after a while; it simply mattered more to me to feel the presence.

To me it seems as though it wasn't long into the project that the energy began to change. After some time, the energy began to speak and advised of its nature, which, quite frankly, was really mind blowing. How it moved, picked up information, left information off, how it looked, interacted—all of it was quite astounding. The fact that it cannot be personified and never had lived a life on the earth, yet had the ability to help us to understand its nature, was a real joy.

This project has given me a sense of being connected to all that is. In fact, it has created a much stronger sense of being connected, as it has shared information that it has picked up about me, my life, my family, my habits, and quirks and has made positive suggestions for change. Information that has been shared was beyond the degree of knowledge that Carole Lynne has about me or parts of my family (for instance, my parents' neighbors).

I feel that as I have worked with this project, my own mediumship has been enhanced, and I have had a change of views in respect to energy. There is a deeper knowing than ever existed before and more of a conviction that Spirit communicates with us in many ways all of the time, if we are sensitive enough to be aware of it.

I have especially felt the tender compassion of the healing that takes place, and I do feel that it is in healing that the project has greater application for others when it comes time to share it publicly. I feel that there are some enlightened few who would well understand the nature of this energy, but many people are not yet ready to try to wrap their understanding around what the Energy is saying about itself. Some aspects of this project have seemed too fantastic to be real, more like science fiction, but one has the awareness that the Energy is more solid, more tangible than we ever knew.

I am excited about the prospects for the project in the future as the Energy brings greater awareness to mankind about it and about the cosmos.

Bob Blake's comments:

The Sitting Project has been a fascinating learning experience for me! I was flattered to be invited to participate in what I saw as an opportunity to observe trance mediumship up close and personal, especially since I am not aware that I have mediumistic abilities. I did fully understand and accept that the latter was a key basis for my involvement. I have been told that I am and can be a good healer, but I have not (yet) demonstrated an ability to "talk" with Spirit directly—something I am very curious about and would like to be able to do. Having received a variety of personal messages from Spirit, ones that I could verify, from a range of mediums, I always go into spirit communication/demonstration opportunities with an open mind and a curiosity to hear from Spirit, as well as to see how accurate any message I might receive may be.

I did not see the Sitting Project as a chance to develop my own mediumistic skills, although I was open to that possibility. My role was to be that of interested, if critical, observer. I did think I might receive messages, and results from our early sessions bore that out. Further, I soon realized that I might get more personalized information than is normally possible in a church message or private reading, since the spirits coming through allowed us to ask questions, not only about the nature of the process, but also of a personal nature.

I have received more information about the process of spirit communication, the nature of the Spirit coming through—both "personified" and "Energy"—and am excited about the experiential nature of the "dialogue" we have been having thus far with Spirit. The most significant "contact" is the most recent "presence"—the "Energy" we cannot personify—which seems as interested in us as we are in it.

It is fascinating to be having such an open dialogue with something I can only imagine and which I cannot personify—indeed which this "Energy" will not allow us to personify—but which impresses me with its obvious intelligence and its all-seeing, all-knowing demeanor. It characterizes itself as the fabric of the universe, of all universes; it was part of the creation and now holds us and the world as we know it together. It provides the life force in our bodies and the structure of our physical surroundings, but it is ethereal, invisible, and has no substance, at least in terms of the "spirits" we are familiar with, of a person we have known and who may choose to "appear" to us through a medium.

When I receive a message from "Spirit," I look for evidence that the "spirit" is someone I knew or can relate to. In the case of our "Energy," I am having to take much on faith. While I am open to the possibility of the existence of something beyond my understanding, it has been a challenge to broaden my understanding beyond what now seems almost "mere" personification. The information received from this "Energy," both contextual and in response to our questions, has seemed understandable and acceptable because it has been logical and in some cases personalized and realizable (e.g., my being "directed" to lost jewelry, or comments/advice related to personal issues not otherwise detailed). Further, we are receiving healing through this process, both by participating and directly from the "Energy," which is a characteristic of the more "familiar" mediumistic experience.

I now look forward to gaining a greater understanding from and of this "Energy" through continued dialogue and working to expand my own consciousness and broaden my experiential abilities. I would like to see additional evidence of what this "Energy" is and does. Such increased awareness of and ability to interact with this

"Energy" can help me learn more about myself and my ability to interact, perhaps, not only with Spirit in all its forms, but also with other people.

At this point, it is unclear just how the Sitting Project might be opened to or shared with other interested people. Obviously the book will be available to introduce the project. And it may be that there could be discussion groups focused on the book, either structured or informal, probably best with small groups. Demonstrations are another avenue, again probably with smaller, controlled groups. In this case, would there want or need to be some concurrence that the "Energy" would, in fact, be amenable to such a program? The reaction to the book will help to confirm interest and options.

The Sitting Project is an ongoing project, and if it continues as it has, there will be many new ideas expressed to us and many experiences that we cannot anticipate. Eventually, I hope to share my channeling experiences with more people through group sittings and through private channeled readings.

PART THREE

The Path Widens

Chapter 10

Sri Aurobindo and the Mother

~~~~~~

MY HUSBAND REMINDS ME that I have to give the credit to my sister-in-law Sharon, as she was the person who wanted to visit the Ashram in Pondicherry when a group of us were making a family trip to southern India. If it had not been for Sharon, perhaps I would never have found the teachings of Sri Aurobindo and the Mother—teachings that are influencing me profoundly. I also have to thank my son, Alan, for marrying Anita Roberts. Anita's father, John Roberts, a native-born Indian who became a Seventh Day Adventist Minister and founded churches throughout India, has arranged for me to meet people from many of India's spiritual traditions. We thank him for arranging a trip for our family to Pondicherry and to the Sri Aurobindo Ashram. If you do not know of Sri Aurobindo and the Mother, the resource section of this book provides a website and e-mail addresses, through which you can learn more about their history, their books, and the work that continues today at the Sri Aurobindo Ashram. What follows is my personal experience with the writings of Sri Aurobindo and the person who founded the Ashram with him, known as "The Mother."

First Trip

~~~~~~~~~~

My first trip to the Ashram in Pondicherry was a bit disappointing for me on a personal level, as I wanted so to sit and meditate near the Samadhi of Sri Aurobindo and the Mother, the white-marble shrine where the bodies of Sri Aurobindo and the Mother are laid at rest. I was with a large group of people and we had just been out to lunch before visiting the Ashram. Most of our large party was more interested in the Ashram as a historical site, and so they were not as motivated to sit for a long time in silence. I am very grateful to those who took us out to lunch and I enjoyed our social time, but part of me yearned to spend more time in the Ashram. The one event that saved this experience for me was a visit to the Ashram bookstore. A woman came over to me and asked me if she could help me pick out some books. I was very happy to have her help, and she picked out a book called *On Himself* by Sri Aurobindo. This book is filled with the correspondence that Sri Aurobindo had with his disciples over many years. These letters have shown me the very frank and intimate way that Sri Aurobindo expresses himself to his disciples.

The woman in the bookstore also picked out several other books. Buying the books was important, but more important was the effect that this woman's presence had on me. I spent a mere fifteen minutes with her, but when I left I realized I had merged with an energy that I had never perceived or felt within me before. This woman clearly had vision that I did not have. Her eyes had an expression of kindness that I will never forget. When I left the Ashram, I knew I had to return to Pondicherry.

Second Trip

Two years later I had the opportunity to take another trip to India, and I visited the Ashram again. During the two years, I had been reading many books by Sri Aurobindo and the Mother, and their teachings were becoming an important part of my own spiritual unfoldment. On this trip my husband and I were able to meet Vijay, who is one of the teachers at the Ashram's Centre of Education. I had been corresponding with him over the Internet whenever I had questions about the books I was reading. When I met Vijay, I found him to be a man with patience and wisdom, and he was in incredibly good physical shape for a man his age. We also met Gita, a lady who works closely with Vijay in the Ashram. I found Gita to be gentle, warm, compassionate, and also in great physical condition. About thirty seconds after I'd met them, both became my role models, and I wanted to be more like them.

This time when I went to the Ashram bookstore, I bought so many books that two boxes had to be shipped back to the United States. And when the boxes arrived at my home in Massachusetts, I was so excited that I could not even open them for a few days. Somehow I knew that once I opened that box, I was opening a new part of my consciousness.

As I have read the books, I have responded deeply to the teachings of Sri Aurobindo and the Mother. It is hard to know where to start as I share my thoughts about why I am so affected by the writings of these two magnificent people, who lived upon this earth and still continue to inspire, help, and guide humanity.

The Independent Thinker

I am drawn to Sri Aurobindo because he was an independent thinker and did most of his spiritual work on his own. On my spiritual journey I have been a bit of a loner, always sidestepping teachers who told me what to do or how to think. It is not that I do not want instruction, but I have never wanted any teacher to try to fit me into a mold. In other words, I do not like a cookie-cutter approach to teaching. I have always sought out teachers who would not try to make me accept their way of thinking, but instead would support me as I struggled to find my own spiritual values. While learning from teachers has been very important to me, it has been my direct experience of the Divine that has been my greatest teacher.

My most important mediumship teacher, Brenda Lawrence, has always told me that she is not really my teacher, but that Spirit is my teacher. She has made it clear that she does not expect me to be like her; I need to be my own medium. I have had other teachers who were too bossy, and I was not able to work with them.

Sri Aurobindo did not receive his deepest spiritual teachings by studying spiritual texts. While the ancient Indian teachings are important to him and part of his spiritual education, from his writings, I perceive that it was his direct relationship with Divine Consciousness that had the greatest influence on his spiritual evolution.

He says that each man has a different spiritual journey, depending on his nature. (I wish he would say "man or woman" or "person," but then he is a product of his generation, like any of the rest of us.) When I read letters to the disciples, I see time and time again that they are not being told what to do, but are encouraged to find out what to do themselves. Sri Aurobindo says in many of his books that to do Integral Yoga, such and such is required, but that a man may follow a variety of spiritual paths and still find God. He is not saying that his yoga is the only path to God; instead, he says Integral Yoga is his path of spiritual development, and if you want to join him, he will lay out quite clearly what is expected.

Sri Aurobindo is like a good parent who teaches a child how to think, not what to think. In this excerpt from *On Himself* (Sri Aurobindo Ashram 1972), he tells about his spiritual education. It is important to note that Sri Aurobindo fought for the independence of India, and so before he and the Mother founded the Ashram, his life was involved with political struggles, which included some time in jail.

I began my yoga in 1904 without a Guru; in 1908 I received important help from a Mahratta Yogi and discovered the foundations of my Sadhana; but from that time till the Mother came to India I received no spiritual help from anyone else. My Sadhana before and afterwards was not founded upon books but upon personal experiences that crowded upon me from within. But in the jail I had the Gita and the Upanishads with me, practiced the yoga of the Gita and meditated with the help of the Upanishads; these were the only books from which I found guidance; the Veda which I first began to read long afterwards in Pondicherry rather confirmed what experiences I already had than was any guide to my Sadhana.

I respond so strongly to his statement that when he began to read the Veda, what he read confirmed his experiences. For me, having a particular kind of spiritual experience and then afterwards reading something that confirms my experience is so much more powerful than reading about a particular kind of spiritual experience first and then having an experience.

Here is another example of Sri Aurobindo's independence. He wrote to a disciple:

> I do not know what X said or in which article, I do not have it with me. But if the statement is that nobody can have a successful meditation or realize anything till he is pure and perfect, I fail to follow it; it contradicts my own experience. I have always had realization by meditation first and purification started afterwards as a result. I have seen many get important, even fundamental realizations by meditation who could not be said to have a great inner development. Are all Yogis who have meditated with effect and had great realizations in their inner consciousness perfect in their nature? It does not look like it to me. I am unable to believe in absolute generalizations in this field, because the development of spiritual consciousness is an exceedingly vast and complex affair in which all sorts of things can happen and one might say that for each man it is different according to his nature and that one thing that is essential is the inner call and aspiration and the perseverance to follow after it no matter how long it takes, what are the difficulties or impediments because nothing else will satisfy the soul within us.
>
> If absolute surrender, faith etc. from the beginning were essential for Yoga, then nobody could do it. I myself could not have done it if such a condition had been demanded of me.

Sri Aurobindo makes it clear that he does not want to make generalizations about spiritual experience. He is also not about to believe something if it is contrary to his experience.

Sri Aurobindo is not intimidated by authority.

The following excerpt from *On Himself* is Sri Aurobindo's response to a disciple's letter about spiritual experiences the disciple is having. Sri Aurobindo writes:

> Your bells etc., mentioned by you as recent experiences were already enumerated as long ago as the time of the Upanishads as signs accompanying the opening to a larger consciousness, *brahmanyabhivyaktikarani yoge*. If I remember right our sparks come in the same list. The fact has been recorded again and again in Yogic literature. I had the same experience hundreds of times in the earlier part of my Sadhana. So you see you are in very honorable company in this matter and need not trouble yourself about the objections of physical science.

These words feel as if they have been written for me. I have had many spiritual experiences that have involved the most beautiful sounds imaginable, including the sounds of bells and gongs. I've also seen sparks of light, particularly in the earlier stages of spiritual development. It would be easy for me to refrain from sharing my spiritual experiences, because I have been brainwashed during my lifetime to disregard any experience that cannot be proved by an authority (i.e., physical science).

Here is an excerpt from *On Himself* in which Sri Aurobindo reacts to a friend who challenges his visions:

> I remember when I first began to see inwardly (and outwardly with the open eye), a scientific friend of mine began to talk of after-images—"these are only after-images!" I asked him whether these after-images remained before the eye for two minutes at a time—he said, "no," to his knowledge only for a few seconds; I also

asked him whether one could get after-images of things not around one or even not existing upon this earth, since they had other shapes, another character, other hues, contours and a very different dynamism, life-movements and values—he could not reply in the affirmative. That is how these so-called scientific explanations break down as soon as you pull them out of their cloudland of mental theory and face them with the actual phenomena they pretend to decipher.

These words of Sri Aurobindo give me permission to honor what I felt intuitively: spiritual experience is not always in the realm of the scientific world. Science does not yet have the instruments or experiments that can prove the validity of my experiences. Spirit speaks to me in many ways, and not all of those ways are measurable and repeatable, as the scientific world demands. While I have great respect for the demands of science, I do not need to disregard my experiences because they cannot fit into current scientific protocol.

Sri Aurobindo's words also speak to my heart because I have had many visions of things that do not appear to me to be of this earth—visions of places, shapes, and beings from other unexplained realms. I do not need to be ashamed or cowardly about my visions. This great teacher gives me great courage.

Allow me to share one more quote from *On Himself,* and then if you are enthralled by his words, perhaps you will order the book and read it in its entirety. In this letter, Sri Aurobindo discusses the difficulty of testing spiritual experiences through scientific methods or even testing within the spiritual community.

It seems to me that no ordinary mind will accept the apparition of Buddha out of a wall or the half hours talk with Hayagriva as valid facts by any kind of testing . . . .

Sri Aurobindo and the Mother

Or how was I to test by the ordinary mind my experience of Nirvana? To what conclusion could I come about it by the aid of the ordinary positive reason? How could I test its validity? I am at a loss to imagine. I did the only thing I could—to accept it as a strong and valid truth of experience, let it have its full play and produce its full experiential consequences until I had sufficient Yogic knowledge to put it in its place. Finally, how without inner knowledge or experience can you or anyone else test the inner knowledge and experience of others?

Asking the seekers on the spiritual path to test and prove all spiritual experiences is like asking us to prove that love, compassion, and sorrow exist. There is a reality that we call the Source, God, the Divine, and many other beloved names; there can never be any physical proof of the existence of this reality. The proof is in the soul of each individual who is able to blend with the many levels of consciousness and, in doing so, at long last discovers the Truth. And then there are also people who, apparently absentmindedly and without any conscious intension, stumble upon great knowledge.

How fortunate we are that Sri Aurobindo was such a prolific writer. One can only wonder how he could have written the large number of books that one finds in the Pondicherry Ashram bookstore. I have a new friend, a teacher who facilitates me in my spiritual growth without telling me how to think or what to believe. I am truly blessed to be surrounded—and I do mean literally surrounded—by such wonderful books. I cannot say that I have felt his spirit around me. Perhaps I will.

Experiencing the Presence of the Mother

As I read the Mother's words in the many books she has written, I know that if I had the good fortune to have been one of her students while she lived upon this earth and taught the children who went to the school at the Pondicherry Ashram, I would have been able to tell her my most precious thoughts. She would not have stepped on and crushed my experiences; instead she would have encouraged me to try to understand my own spiritual experiences and learn from them in my own unique way.

The last time I was in Pondicherry, I spoke with a person who was a student of the Mother's throughout his childhood. He told me the following:

> I was a child, but I remember the Mother so distinctly. She was more than what a human mother could be, and we went to her for every little thing. At the same time, we had the faith that she was much more, that she was Divine. She took a class in French for little children where she told us stories through beautifully illustrated books, gave us small little poems to learn by heart, which we recited in front of her, and answered all the questions that we could have on any topic under the sun. And the love which poured forth was boundless.

I envy this man who was able to study with the Mother and be in her presence. However, I am grateful that I am able to learn from the many writings she left us and from her energy as it comes to those of us who call out for her.

I have felt the spirit of the Lady who founded the Ashram with Sri Aurobindo. Perhaps I feel the spirit of the Mother around me more easily because she is an artist and a poet. I have always been drawn to artists and can easily recognize the energy of the artist. Perhaps I feel spirit of the Mother around me because she is an excellent teacher as well, having spent many years developing the education department at the Pondicherry Ashram. First and foremost, I am a teacher, and so is the Mother. I easily find the Mother to be a soul mate.

Forgive me if I speak of her in such familiar terms, but that is how I respond to the words of the Mother and the pictures of the Mother. I have the sense that I have always known her. It took me two years of reading books by Sri Aurobindo before I could begin to understand his teachings. It took a long time for me to get to know him. But whenever I read words by the Mother, it is as if I have read them before and they have always been part of me. She is so easy to understand, so practical, and one of the wisest souls I have ever encountered.

The Mother's Words and Views

As a Spiritualist, I have views that correspond with the views of the Mother. While we do not have any dogma or creed in Spiritualism, we do have a set of principles to contemplate and live by, and the seventh is the principle of personal responsibility: "We affirm the moral responsibility of the individual and that one's happiness or unhappiness is the result of obedience or disobedience to Nature's physical and spiritual laws." Also in Spiritualism, thoughts *are* things, and they do change our lives. In the following excerpt of the Mother's words, she also expresses how we are responsible for our consciousness and can change our consciousness if we have the aspiration to do so.

The Mother had been asked by a student, "How can we empty the consciousness of its mixed contents?" For me, another way of asking this question would be, "How can one get rid of things one does not want within one's consciousness?" The Mother's answer is:

> By aspiration, the rejection of the lower movements, a call to a higher force. If you do not accept certain movements, then naturally, when they find that they can't manifest, gradually they diminish in force and stop occurring. If you refuse to express everything that is of a lower kind, little by little the very thing disappears, and the consciousness is emptied of lower things. It is by refusing to give expression—I mean not only in action but also in thought, in feeling. When impulses, thoughts, emotions come, if you refuse to express them, if you push them aside and remain in a state of inner aspiration and calm, then gradually they lose their force and stop coming. So the consciousness is emptied of its lower movements.
>
> But for instance, when undesirable thoughts come, if you look at them, observe them, if you take pleasure in following them in their movements, they will never stop coming. It is the same thing when you have undesirable feelings or sensations: if you pay attention to them, concentrate on them or even look at them with a certain indulgence, they will never stop. But if you absolutely refuse to receive and express them, after some time they stop. You must be patient and very persistent.
>
> —*Collected Works of the Mother Centenary Edition* 6 Sri Aurobindo Ashram 1976

As I read these words, a vision comes to me of the people I know who make their lives miserable by complaining all the time. They never find joy in life because they willfully hang on to negative memories. I don't mean to imply that when something bad happens we should deny it. I am the first person to advocate the expression of our feelings, seeing a therapist when necessary, and attending all kinds of support group programs. But there comes a time to let go of negative experiences and move on.

Some people enjoy the drama of gossip. Gossips also like to complain about how terrible their lives are and how terrible everyone else's life is. The perceptions of life through the eyes of the gossips are very sad indeed. The Mother points out, as do our Spiritualist teachers, that we are all responsible for our own thoughts. We do not have to entertain negative thoughts. We can have negative thoughts, but once aware of them, we need to deal with our thoughts quickly and let them go.

As a teacher within the Spiritualist community, I have had a hard time trying to tell certain students to let go of negativity. And as a medium who works regularly with people who are in deep grief over the passing of loved ones, I have a hard time talking honestly to clients who are so angry over the passing of a loved one that they are ruining their own lives and jeopardizing the lives of all those who are close to them. The Mother's direct words to her students support me as a teacher who must learn to talk more directly to those in my classes and spiritual circles.

I also fall into negative thinking patterns. The words of the Mother and the teachings in the Spiritualist community are like lifeboats for me when I feel I am drowning in self-pity. For instance, this year I am coping with quite a bit of pain in my left shoulder, which has been diagnosed as slightly frozen. I do not have full range of motion, and there are days when I am quite uncomfortable. Having received good medical care, I am still not able to do everything I could do a year ago. Sometimes I let it ruin my day, and other times I fully accept the nuisance, but continue on and have an incredible day. My shoulder is the same a lot of the time; the difference between a good day or a bad day is my attitude. My thoughts make the difference.

President Harry Truman's quote, "The buck stops here," captures how we in the United States might express our ideas of personal responsibility. As I use that expression and pound gently on my own chest, what I am saying is that I am the one who is responsible for what happens to me. Of course, there are exceptions. If you and I are on a train that crashes with another train, we cannot blame ourselves for that accident. But most days we are not on a crashing train; most days we have a great influence over what happens! The Mother says:

There are human beings also who indulge in vice—one vice or another, like drinking or drug-injections—and who know very well that this is leading them to destruction and death. But they choose to do it, knowingly.

Que.: They have no control over themselves.

There is always a moment when everyone has self-control. And if one had not said "Yes" once, if one had not taken the decision, one would not have done it.

There is not one human being who has not the energy and capacity to resist something imposed upon him—if he is left free to do so. People tell you, "I can't do otherwise"—it is because in the depths of their heart they *do not want* to do otherwise; they have accepted to be the slaves of their vice. There is a moment when one accepts.

—*CWMCE* 8 Sri Aurobindo Ashram 1976

How true, how true! There is a moment when one accepts an alcoholic drink that one should not have, an illegal drug, a plate of food one knows one is allergic to, a sexual adventure that goes against one's moral values, or a bribe one should not take. There is a moment of decision when one decides to rob someone, kill someone, or tell a lie. There is also a moment when one makes the right decision. It is almost always our choice.

Sri Aurobindo and the Mother

The Mother, like Sri Aurobindo, respects the spiritual experience of the individual. In her book, *The Mother's Vision* (Sri Aurobindo Ashram 2002), she says:

> When one is truly and exclusively turned to the spiritual Truth, whatever name may be given to it, when all the rest becomes secondary, when that alone is imperative and inevitable, then, one single moment of intense, absolute, total concentration is enough to receive the answer.
>
> . . . It is good for you, that is all that is needed. If you want to impose it on others, whatever it may be, even if it is perfect in itself, it becomes false.

We cannot impose our spiritual experiences or ideas on other people. They have to have their own experiences. Even as teachers, authors, or public speakers, we can only share our own experiences with those who ask or choose to listen.

Surely many of you have had the same horrendous experiences I had when I have shared my deepest experiences with people who did not really want to hear what I had to offer. Those people either insisted on interpreting my experience in a totally different way, or they interrupted me so that they could tell their own story. In those moments, I would have done anything to take back my words. I am now very cautious about sharing my experiences in a casual conversation.

In the following excerpt from *The Mother's Vision*, the Mother expresses her thoughts on religions and their attempts to organize spiritual experience.

> That is why religions are always mistaken—always— because they want to standardize the expression of an

experience and impose it on everyone as an irrefutable truth. The experience was true, complete in itself, convincing—for the one who had it. The formulation he made of it was excellent—for himself. But to want to impose it on others is a fundamental error, which has altogether disastrous consequences, always, which always leads far, very far from the Truth.

That is why all the religions, however beautiful they may be, have always led man to the worst excesses. All the crimes, the horrors perpetrated in the name of religion are among the darkest stains on human history, and simply because of this initial little error: wanting what is true for one individual to be true for the mass or collectivity.

The Sri Aurobindo Ashram is not a religious but a spiritual community. While I am part of the religion of Spiritualism, I find it to be a religion that does not try to control my thinking. I am an ordained minister and proud to be so. I love this religion that I have chosen to be part of, because there is no formal dogma or creed. The only thing one must say to be a Spiritualist is that one believes in life after death. Spiritualism is founded on the principle of eternal life. We believe, and prove through our demonstrations of spirit communication, that when a person leaves the body, the consciousness continues on within the world of spirit.

Within Spiritualism we have members who believe in reincarnation and those who do not; we have members who are learning a great deal about other religions and philosophies and members who do not care to explore any other religious beliefs. I am an example of a Spiritualist minister who is learning a great deal about the philosophy of Sri Aurobindo and the Mother, and within my religion I am free to explore the ideas of other religions, teachers, philosophers, and spiritual communities.

I agree with the Mother's concerns about religion, and I am happy that I have found a religion that does not step on my experiences or ideas.

My Relationship to the Mother Evolving

In November of 2007, I did quite a bit of reading about Sri Aurobindo and the Mother. One night as I was falling to sleep, I had a vision of the wheel symbol that is used with writings of the Mother. I had not read what the symbol represented, but when I was in Pondicherry, I had bought a metal replica of it. From what I understand, the Mother spoke of this symbol as a flower with two rows of petals—four on the inside and twelve on the outside. Like me, some perceive the symbol as a wheel.

My vision clearly showed a brass or copper wheel spinning and shining very brightly. As the vision appeared, I tried to control it to see if it was a figment of my imagination, but I could not. The wheel was turning; it would face me, turn and show me a side view of itself, and then turn at an angle where I could see only part of it. The wheel kept spinning, and I had this beautiful feeling. I knew that I was having a special experience and perhaps a special communication. After a while, this shimmering wheel was gone from my mind.

For the next few days, I tried to recreate this vision in my mind in order to see if I could imagine it. The fact that I could not proved to me the vision was not something I alone could create.

Seeing the wheel, for me, was a sign that the sphere of truth that I associate with the Mother is supporting me in the writing that I am doing now about Sri Aurobindo and the Mother. I offer a prayer of gratitude to Sri Aurobindo and the Mother for the books they have left us.

Note: I have never met Sri Aurobindo, and I consider myself a new student of his work. I do not represent his teachings; the teachings of the cofounder of the Ashram, known as the Mother; or the Ashram in any manner. What I have shared is my personal experience with the writings of Sri Aurobindo and the Mother, which is part of the way I believe that Spirit has guided me in my spiritual unfoldment.

Chapter 11

The Path of Direct Initiation

~~~~~~

WHAT IS AN INITIATION? When we think of the word *initiation,* we usually imagine a person receiving an initiation from some other person in the name of an organization or in the name of a spiritual source. For example, one might receive an initiation when joining a social club or a spiritual organization. The Merriam-Webster online dictionary defines *initiation* as "a: the act or the instance of initiating; b: the process of being initiated; c: the rites, ceremonies, ordeals, or instructions with which one is made a member of a sect or society or is invested with a particular function or status."

I have participated in a number of formal ceremonies in which I became invested with a particular status or a member of an organization or society. My baptism, confirmation, marriage, and ordination as a Spiritualist minister come to mind. In these formal initiations, an authority figure, such as a teacher, professor, or minister, gave me a blessing, instructions, or vows to repeat.

Along with these formal initiation ceremonies, I have also had spiritually transformative experiences that involved no human being other than me. In these experiences, I received what I name "a direct initiation" from a higher source. I felt my Greater

Self merge with and receive a blessing from the Divine. All of the formal spiritual ceremonies meant a great deal to me, but none of them resulted in the same depth of communication with Divine Consciousness as the direct initiation. The communications between my Greater Self and the Divine that I had on my own have been more sacred and extremely life changing.

It took time for me to decide what to call these transformative experiences. I wanted to call them "spiritual attunements," as each experience has marked the beginning of deeper and more committed work on the spiritual path. However, it feels more precise to call these experiences "initiations."

How do I dare to use such words as *attunement* and *initiation* without the sanction of a teacher, guru, priest, or some other authority? I am scaring myself with such talk! There is a part of me that finds using these words preposterous, egocentric, and downright rebellious. Yet I must listen to another part of my consciousness: that part that can come through to me only when I put my intellect to sleep and allow the spiritual creative flow within me to operate. This part of me says, "Carole Lynne, you are having a direct initiation from the Divine, not because this is some kind of special privilege, but because direct initiation *is* one of the important spiritual paths, and you are asked to experience the Path of Direct Initiation and teach it to others. While many equally useful spiritual paths have teachers who give initiations to their students, not every soul on earth is meant to join a spiritual organization or follow a guru. Some souls are in need of another kind of path. Yes, there will be important teachers on the Path of Direct Initiation, but these teachers are more like facilitators who help to create spiritual environments where people can realize who they are and come to a time when they can communicate with the Divine directly. Carole Lynne, you are meant to walk this path and teach it to others."

The Path of Direct Initiation

The Path of Direct Initiation can include many different kinds of spiritual experiences, including visions, dreams, and visits from spiritual guides and loved ones who have passed over. What is core to the experience is a feeling of having been initiated and moving into a deeper understanding of the spiritual realms.

A Vision of Fire: An Initiatory Experience

I would like to share several initiatory experiences with you. One occurred during a channeling session when I was visiting my mother in her home in Maui. The following is an excerpt from the session. Interspersed in the transcript are my parenthetical remarks to help the reader understand the context.

CAROLE LYNNE STILL IN HER OWN VOICE: I request my highest guidance. I accept no other than the highest energy for the sake of myself and others. I am in Hawaii at my mother's home.

(I begin to have a vision and describe what I am seeing, as if I were a reporter.)

CAROLE LYNNE STILL IN HER OWN VOICE: I am seeing a vision of fire—a huge fire—and out of the fire I see a woman emerging—(she is) white, it looks like me. In this vision of myself I am almost translucent, silvery. Now I see this counterpart of myself coming toward me. Perhaps it is she who wishes to speak to me this morning. I will repeat the words I hear in my mind.

(As I make this statement, I am beginning to go into an altered state of consciousness. I begin to hear words and repeat what I hear. I am hearing words from a level of my own consciousness as it connects with Divine Consciousness. One part of me is therefore speaking to another part of myself.)

GREATER SELF: Carole, you are undergoing and you have been undergoing purification by fire. You are in the last stages, and now you will go to a new level. It is a very joyous level. Do not be afraid. You will not move away from people, but instead you will move closer to people, because your compassion will go to another level and your judgments will all fall away. You will simply see people as beings of light following their own path.

Do not be disturbed by the outburst that you had with your friend Susan. It is part of your earthly nature. But that part of you will fall away soon, and you won't have reactions like that. Susan is her own soul and will follow her path the way she needs to, just as you will follow yours.

Today is the initiation that you have been waiting for. Your channeling teacher cannot initiate you. Your Guidance cannot initiate you. Even the trainings in Reiki that you will receive cannot truly initiate you. It is the other parts of yourself that will perform the initiation, and so I, as part of your Greater Self, have appeared to you today, because it is ultimately the parts of your Greater Self that are connected to all of the universe that will perform the initiations that you must trust and follow. Do not feel a loss when your Guidance does not speak with you all the time. It is the wish of your Guidance that you discover your Greater Self, which is ultimately connected with the essence of your Guidance.

(Now I begin to report what I am seeing in my vision.)

CAROLE LYNNE IN HER OWN VOICE: I feel myself moving down a long tunnel. Within my Greater Self, an angel who will emerge from the fire is hovering over me, taking this trip with me. And now we are coming out of the tunnel. We are on the earth, but the earth looks very different. It has many different levels. It is many worlds going on at the same time. An angel is with me. I am able to absorb all of these worlds. And in this new world that I am seeing, my senses are quite different. My hearing is sensitive, my sight is sensitive, and my nose is sensitive. All of my senses are acute. Plus my sixth sense is starting to develop a whole world of its own within myself where I can see it, I can trust it. I can allow this sense to be part of my regular everyday perception, without having to think of it as a psychic experience.

And now I see myself in a forest, almost like a Goldilocks character, and a big scary bear is coming into the picture. And I am simply passing right through the bear. I am not afraid.

And now I see myself being showered with incredible energies. At first it looked like flowers, it looked like jewels, but it is actually incredible energy that is coming to me, surrounding my whole physical body. I am seeing inside my body. I am seeing this energy going in and breaking up any places where the energy is not moving, any dark spaces.

I see many spiritual masters pass before me—Mary and Jesus, Guru Mai, all those who have touched me.

Now I wish to send the beauty of this energy to my mother, who is in many ways hurting, but there is a side of her that is very beautiful and very spiritual, very insightful. And I appeal to that side of her with this energy.

In this session I learned how the Divine is helping me and encouraging me to stop depending on teachers and even on what I would think of as "spiritual guides." The Divine is letting me know that there is a spark within me that I call my Greater Self or Higher Self, which connects directly with Divine Consciousness. Through this spark, I can receive guidance. All of us have that spark that connects to the Divine, and as we unfold spiritually, we can get more in touch with the guidance from within.

"Today is the initiation that you have been waiting for. Your channeling teacher cannot initiate you. Your Guidance cannot initiate you": these words are the cornerstone in the Path of Direct Initiation. In so many spiritual practices, a teacher or an au-

thority figure gives out initiations when it is felt the student is
ready. On the Path of Direct Initiation there is no authority figure
to make decisions about when the student is ready to receive an
initiation and take the next step on the spiritual path. The student
has to develop an inner knowing and a relationship with Divine
Consciousness that allows him or her to know when a direct initiation has occurred. In fact, the student may not even call this
spiritual event an initiation. No label is necessary. The student
will just know that he or she has walked through another spiritual
door and is closer to Divine Consciousness than before. (I am using the word *initiation* because I need words to communicate my
ideas. But within myself, I do not need to label this experience.)

"[I]t is ultimately the parts of your Greater Self that are connected to all of the universe that will perform the initiations that
you must trust and follow." With these words, I understood that
the part of me that I call my Greater Self or Higher Self is connected to Divine Consciousness and that I must learn to trust
this sacred part of myself. This is true for every human being;
anyone who aspires to understanding the Truth can open up and
be conscious of all of the levels of knowledge that exist. Learning
to trust the sacred part of myself is challenging. I suspect I am not
alone in this difficulty as many readers have questions about their
spiritual experiences, often wondering, as I do, about the images
and sensations that occur as we connect with Divine Consciousness. We ask ourselves "Is this real?"

The Spiritual Imagination

Imagination is a frightening word for many on the spiritual path,
who constantly question whether an experience is real or imagined. Unfortunately, many do not understand what an important
role the imagination plays as we communicate with the Divine.

Ask yourself, what does the imagination do? The imagination constructs images. It is our imagination that allows us to construct images that best express the parts of ourselves that are the Greater Self, a spark of Divine Consciousness. As human beings, the images that come to us help us to understand our own divinity. The images within the spiritual realm we are entering have a reality within that realm.

It was very powerful for me to experience visions of jewels and flowers as the images of these things transformed into pure energy. It was as if I had been taken to a deeper level within my experience where I could see behind the images of the jewels and flowers. While the jewels and flowers have a reality within the spiritual realm, I realized that the ultimate reality was in the energy within the images. Realizing that the images were not literal did not make the visions any less important or authentic; in fact, I understood the visions to be a language that the energies of the universe could use to speak to me. Visions, like beautiful paintings or pictures on billboards, speak to us. They get our attention. They provoke thoughts and feelings. Our visions instruct us and guide us. Our visions also carry spiritual vibrations as a pitcher carries water. The images bathe our souls with their vibrations as the pitcher's water can bathe our physical bodies. When you have visions, let them speak to you and teach you. Let them bathe you with their beauty. Experience the deeper meanings.

How is it that the mystics, the great religious leaders, the poets, the writers, and the artists have all expressed themselves differently when it comes to talking about God, the Divine, and a Power Greater Than Ourselves? The answer is that ultimately Divine Consciousness is beyond words, beyond description, and beyond the understanding of human beings. The part of each one of us that is a spark of the Divine receives knowledge and then expresses that knowledge; the expressions will be different, based on the culture we come from, the age we are living in, and the temperament of each of our personalities. However different our expression, the Divine Consciousness we are all connecting with is the same. Our visions and our expressions of the Divine may differ, but the Divine is what *it* is.

Images Are Controversial

You may not want to hear these words if you want to believe that my vision of the angel is literally true. And if you believe in a religion that says that its beliefs are the only way God can be understood, you may not like hearing that we all perceive the Divine in our own way and that the Divine can initiate people directly.

Or if you believe you have a spirit guide named Jack who wears a Chicago Cubs baseball hat, you may not want to hear how our imagination creates images we can understand. While it may be true that your spirit guide's name is Jack, and it may be true that he wears a Chicago Cubs baseball hat, it may also be true that when you connect with the Divine, your mind interprets this energy as a guide named Jack who wears a baseball hat. And it may be true that someone else who connects with the Divine will instead interpret this energy as a beautiful angel. Perhaps my angel and Jack are the same, but we experience this Divine energy differently. The fact that our images may not be literally true does not in any way take away from the sacredness of the energy that we are merging with. Divine Consciousness is so mystical that it is beyond words and beyond images of any kind. Therefore, as we communicate directly with Divine Consciousness, we have to receive this energy in visions and with words that each of us, as individuals, can comprehend.

Images of Spiritual Guides

Does this mean that there are no spirit guides who are exactly who they say they are? I do believe that there are spirits of those who have passed over and who are able to project images of themselves as they used to be. The spirit of a monk that you perceive may have really lived the life of a monk. However, a guide who presents himself as a monk may continue on with his own spiritual evolution and evolve and merge more deeply with the Divine. Then he may not see himself as a monk any longer, as he will no longer need that image of himself. However, he may still project the image of a monk to you, if you need an image in order to receive his teachings. At this point he may be a sphere of light and knowledge, but he is projecting an image of himself as he was when he lived on the earth. Or you may be creating the image of the monk yourself, as you need an image in order to receive the energy of knowledge.

Images of Our Loved Ones

When our loved ones from spirit communicate with us, most of them are still at a point in their spiritual evolution where they need images of themselves as they used to be. And most of us also need these images in order to differentiate between the spirit of our grandmother and our sister. If our grandmother and sister appeared to us a spheres of light, how would we know who is who? As a medium receiving messages from those in spirit, I need to see images of the spirits as they used to be when they were alive, so that I can describe these images to my clients. But I do not feel that our loved ones are as they used to be; I believe they are evolving in eternal life and merging with the Divine.

Perhaps in time the spirits of our loved ones will evolve to a realm where they, like our higher guides, merge with Divine Consciousness in a way that they no longer need images of themselves as individuals. And perhaps we as human beings will evolve to the point where we know the spirits of our loved ones are with us even if we do not receive images of them. We will simply feel their presence. They will be communicating with us in a different way.

The Story of the Lettuce: An Initiatory Experience

One of my most important initiations occurred when my husband Marlowe was working in New York City in 1987. He had just begun working for the Macmillan Publishing Company. We still maintained our family home in Massachusetts, and the company provided us with a small apartment in New York. I visited Marlowe every couple of weeks. One night, as I was in our apartment, preparing dinner for a small group, I was washing some lettuce. All of a sudden, the small separate kitchen area and the lettuce lit up. I continued to wash the lettuce as it sparkled. I was at peace. Transfixed in that moment, I noticed that the leaves of lettuce looked like a flower or a small cabbage. I gazed at the shimmering leaves, and I was taken to another realm. In amazement I stood there, knowing that I had entered a new door of awareness—a door that would bring me into a new state of consciousness.

I did not tell anyone about my experience. Who would believe that my whole life changed as a head of lettuce lit up? But I thought about my vision for days. Whenever I look back to see what event transported me to the spiritual arena I am traveling within today, I see that moment in the small kitchen. I can still retrieve the image, as it has become part of my deep memory and is embedded in my soul energy. Perhaps my vision is what many call a moment of enlightenment.

Available for Anyone Who Aspires

Revelations are part of our spiritual culture. All revelations are received directly from the Divine by a human being, who then shares what he or she has learned. All the great religions and spiritual texts have come from the same source, but each human being who received them did so through his or her own state of consciousness, which was somewhat colored by cultural background and personal experience. All spiritual seekers who have received revelations received them directly and interpreted the energy of Truth that has come to them. They have given form to the light of Truth. They have created images and words to express these teachings to other human beings.

When I have received a direct initiation, I have felt spiritual teachings being imparted to me or the Divine reaching me through a vision or a dream. I have felt that a part of my consciousness has been opened to a point where Divine energy can flow in. I have no monopoly on this experience. It is there for anyone who aspires to be closer to the Divine.

Sometimes direct initiations come in the form of waking visions. I had such a waking vision in 2007. In the previous chapter, "Sri Aurobindo and the Mother," you read about my vision of the wheel-like symbol for the Mother. When I first saw this symbol, it was another initiation experience for me. The vision represented a new cycle in my spiritual growth. It is still too soon to know what the ramifications of this new cycle or step in my spiritual path are. Why do I see this vision as an initiation?

Let us go back to the definition of *initiation:* "Instructions with which one is made a member of a sect or society or is invested with a particular function or status." As I contemplate this definition and the vision of the wheel, I see that this vision represents drawing closer to the consciousness of the Mother. For two years I have been reading about her and reading books that she has written and transcripts of lectures she has given. But now, with the vision of her symbol, I feel that I am taking some very tiny baby steps toward the Mother, blending with her consciousness in a new way. Another way of looking at this experience, and perhaps a more honest evaluation, would be to say that I am discovering the consciousness of the Mother within my own consciousness, as ultimately we are all part of the same great consciousness. The spiritual path is really about discovering that we are part of Divine Consciousness and therefore all connected energetically. I am discovering that all the great masters exist within me, within you, within All That Is. We must all be open to this discovery.

Take My Labels with a Grain of Salt

As I have written about my direct initiations, I am attempting to organize spiritual experiences and stick a label on them, when these experiences cannot truly be condensed and refined into a quantity that can carry a label. I ask readers to use my labels loosely, knowing that what I have experienced is really beyond words. When I speak of having had a moment of enlightenment, please do not take my words literally, as there ultimately are no words for what I experienced. In the end, you must have your own experiences and find your own words to describe the teachings that come to you.

Trying to explain spiritual knowledge in written language often takes many volumes, as the knowledge is flowing through the mind of the writer, who may feel the need to express his or her ideas in many variations. Even though we can learn a great deal from great written works, the knowledge still cannot be contained, no matter how few or how many words are written or spoken. The Divine simply cannot be contained within our mental structures.

Ultimate knowledge is wordless. The part of each one of us that is a spark of Divine Consciousness is able to merge with the Divine. In those special moments we receive guidance, we receive healing, and sometimes the moment brings us a feeling of having received a spiritual attunement or initiation.

Our words to describe those moments will always fall short of the Truth.

Chapter 12

I Found the Ankh, the Ankh Found Me

~~~~~~~~~~~~~~~~~~

HUMAN BEINGS USE MANY METHODS to communicate with each other. We use language, physical gestures and facial expressions, and pictures. Some of the pictures become symbols that we use time and time again. For instance, when you are driving in the United States and see a stop sign, you know that you need to stop, not only because of the word *stop* on the sign, but because of the shape and color of the sign. Wherever you drive, the stop sign looks the same. Another symbol is the dollar sign ($). We all know that this symbol means "money."

When the world of spirit communicates with us, it also uses symbols, but the symbols are not the same for everyone. Sometimes a person can be drawn to a certain symbol and not know why; one feels that a particular word, number, color, or image has a mysterious quality or a spiritual energy connected to it. For instance, the number seven has become a spiritual symbol for me, simply because I have felt drawn to that number again and again since I was a little child.

The symbols received while on the spiritual path are often unique to the individual who is receiving them. And traditional and well-known images, such as a seashell, may have a totally untraditional meaning to the individual receiving the image while on the spiritual path. For one person, the shell may signify an incredible trip taken with a loved one, while for another the shell may symbolize the outer personality that we ultimately shed when we are born again into new phases of our lives. And to another the shell may simply be symbolic of the sea.

Symbols are personal and ultimately can be transforming. It is no wonder that as the highest part of our consciousness merges with Divine Consciousness, the language through which we communicate is often symbolic.

The symbol of the ankh has played a part in my life three times: as a child developing mystical feelings, as an adult signing my first publishing contract, and then as a medium receiving a mystical direct initiation in Edinburgh, Scotland.

I Found the Ankh

One day when I was nine years old, I was at an outdoor fair full of booths selling all kinds of wonderful and imaginative things: jewelry, candles, and beautiful handmade gifts. I was walking along, and all of a sudden it was as if my eyes became a laser beam that instantly landed on a piece of jewelry. It was a pendant with an oval shape at the top, and from the bottom of the oval flowed a long stem. I had no idea what this piece of jewelry was, but to this day, I remember seeing it and feeling desperate to have it. I just knew it belonged to me. My parents bought it for me, and I kept it hidden away in my jewelry box. For me, this piece was a symbol of something very mysterious and special. I did not have any questions about what it was or what its significance was. I was just a little girl who had found something magical—my special piece that I needed to guard and keep safe.

In my twenties I realized that what I had bought as a child was an ankh, which for the Egyptians is the symbol for life. Now I knew its spiritual significance. But in my twenties I was not particularly interested in spirituality, so I forgot about my ankh, and it stayed in my now scuffed-up and tired-looking childhood jewelry box.

The Ankh Brings My First Publishing Contract

When I was in my sixties, the ankh found me in the form of a publishing company. I had been asked to attend a publishing meeting because of my experience with New Age books. By this time I was a working psychic medium and a musician composing and recording songs related to spiritual themes. After this meeting, I gave Jan Johnson from Weiser Books a copy of my CD called *Dare to Be Happy.* Jan loved the music and a few weeks later asked me to compose a CD of chants that would be paired with a book of affirmations and prayers.

As we talked, Jan put three or four Weiser books on the coffee table. I noticed the Weiser logo on all of these books and started to shiver. There was the ankh, the logo for Weiser Books, one of the oldest and most respected metaphysical book publishing companies. It would not be long before I would sign my first publishing contract with Red Wheel/Weiser and produce the book and CD called *Heart and Sound.*

The ankh had found me.

A Mystical Initiation in Edinburgh, Scotland

The next time the ankh found me was in 2001, when I made my first trip to work at the Edinburgh College of Parapsychology. I had been studying for the past six years in the United States with the American Federation of Spiritualist Churches and taking some courses at the Arthur Findlay College in Stansted, England. I had finished many of my American certifications, and now it was time to finish my English courses. Part of the work in my European course was to serve in four Spiritualist church services in England to demonstrate that I was a competent public speaker and medium. In 2001 my last test service was scheduled to take place just before I was to work for a week in Edinburgh. This service was to be held at a Darlington church. Nora Shaw helped to set up the board of teachers who would judge my work.

Notice an important spiritual coincidence. You may remember Nora Shaw from chapter 1. She was the teacher at Stansted whose words of wisdom convinced me that I should become an evidential medium before allowing the public to read the transcripts of my channeling sessions. Now here I was in 2001, about to take a mediumship test service that she had arranged for me. And it was because of Nora's recommendation that I would be leaving to work at the Edinburgh College of Parapsychology the day after my exam. Nora, most likely without knowing it consciously, became instrumental in helping me reach my spiritual destiny.

I took the test in Darlington, and as I worked on the platform, the world of spirit was there for me. The evidence that came through was very good that evening, and I passed the exam. The next day my husband and I left for Edinburgh. Angela McInnes, a well-known medium in the United Kingdom and the teacher who invited me to work at the college, and her husband, Magnus McInnes, offered to take us to the now well-known church called Rosslyn Chapel, in Rosslyn, Scotland. (The reason I say "now well-known" is because since the book and movie *The Da Vinci Code* came out, this chapel can barely hold all the visitors that come to see where an important scene in the book takes place. I was fortunate to visit Rosslyn Chapel before it became a pop-culture spiritual site.) When I made my first visit, I could still feel the energy of the ancient times. I felt an incredible energy, and the symbol of the ankh was a vision in my mind. (There are numerous symbols carved on the wall of this chapel; the ankh may be one of them, and that is why it came into my mind.) I had no idea how interesting and important the vision of the ankh was going to be to me until a few nights later, when George Cornick, the secretary of the Edinburgh College of Parapsychology, presented me with a welcoming gift in front of the whole staff. As he handed me a book called *Rosslyn: Guardian of the Secrets of the Holy Grail* by Tim Wallace-Murphy and Marilyn Hopkins, he had no idea that he was acting as a spiritual messenger and that this book contained passages of great significance to me as a spiritual seeker.

When I received this book, it almost shook in my hands. I knew there was an inner meaning to this gift, but did not comprehend what was about to happen. Images of my visit to Rosslyn Chapel kept floating through my mind, and I kept leafing through the pages of the book, looking for clues. What in this book had special significance for me? Why was I given this book? Nothing I read seemed relevant.

Frustration was welling up within me, and I retreated from the group and went into the medium's quarters. I sat down on my bed, and within my mind, I cried, "Spirit, why did you give me this book? Right now, I am going to open this book and then put my finger on a paragraph. I want the answer to be there. I want the words that I read to suggest why I have been given a book that I am having such a strong reaction to." If it sounds like I was being demanding of Spirit, I was. I had an intense desire to put words to an incredible experience that started with the energy at Rosslyn Chapel—an experience that was now doubling and tripling in its intensity as I held this book in my hands.

I opened the book and quickly put the index finger of my right hand on a paragraph. Here is what I read:

> Admission to the ultimate mysteries of Saphenath Pancah, revealed at the seventh and final degree, was granted at the twin temples of Behedet and Heliopolis which represented the dual attributes necessary for awakening of the crown chakra. These were the ultimate centres of illumination into the pure knowledge of God that was held to be beyond all understanding. Attainment of this degree was far from automatic: the candidate had to be of such outstanding merit that he could be invited by the pharaoh with the full consent of the Inner Fraternity. There was a grand reception for the invited candidate, followed by a public procession, after which an assembly of the initiates was held during the hours of darkness in purpose-built houses called Maneras. Here the new member of the illuminati was given an ambrosial drink of the gods known as Omellas, and was told that he had finally arrived at the end of all proofs. He was invested with the insignia of the Ankh. . . .

As I read those words, I had one of those mystical experiences where you know that the words you are reading are meant to be read at this exact moment. I was being invested with the ankh, my spiritual symbol since childhood, because I had just taken test after test after test where I had to bring proof after proof after proof that I was communicating with those in spirit. I was this "initiate," and I had "arrived at the end of all proofs"—the end of a long road that had included written courses, many exams, and test services in both the United States and England. And to top it all off, this passage brought my spiritual number seven to me as it spoke of the "seventh and final degree." For me, this experience was not a coincidence, but a spiritual reward.

After reading this passage, I stumbled back into the tearoom and socialized with the group again, never telling them that I was in the middle of an epiphany.

Longing for Gold

While I had been spiritually invested with the image of an ankh, I did not have a physical representation of this symbol in my hands. Back in my childhood jewelry box still lay the original, cheaply made ankh my parents had bought me at that neighborhood fair. But as I sat in the medium's quarters at the Edinburgh College, I wanted a solid gold ankh that I could wear around my neck. In fact, I had been searching for one for several years. Every time I found a store that had ankh pendants, they were made out of silver.

Within several days of receiving my message from the Rosslyn Chapel book, my golden ankh found me. I attended a lecture about all the powerful mediums who had lived in the Edinburgh area. After the lecture, Nora and I went into the tearoom, and because both of us are mediums, we were seated at the mediums' table with the speaker, Nita Saunders. As the three of us chatted, I had the feeling that Nita could help me find my ankh of gold. I was not quite sure how to bring up the subject, but at one point, like a true American, I just launched into it.

"Nita, I am not quite sure why I am telling you this, but I have been looking for an ankh made of gold for many years. Do you know where I can get one?"

She said, "I certainly do. There is a jeweler who lives almost next door to me, and he makes ankhs out of gold."

I felt as if I were in the middle of a marvelous fairy tale. The next day Nita called the college with the name of the jeweler and his contact information, and Marlowe and I boarded a bus out to his small town to take a look. Within several days, my ankh of gold was ready, and we went back and picked it up. I had my prize and felt that it had been given to me by the world of spirit. It was my graduation gift after passing all my exams in the United States and Europe. It was perfect.

On the spiritual path there are symbols that emerge for us over and over again. Some could call this repetition mere coincidence. Others of us know that sometimes it is not a simple coincidence, but a mystically emerging energy that somehow brings a symbol to us over and over again. We recognize our special symbols as they have a shimmering light around them. They arrive on our doorsteps, like beautiful birds that knew where they were going and have simply flown home.

Chapter 13

Voices Echoing Voices Echoing Voices

~~~~~~~~~~~~~~~~~~~~~~~~~~~~~~~~~~~

EVEN THOUGH WE EXPLORE spirituality alone and in our own way, the experiences we have and ideas we form are often similar to those of others, confirming that we are all tapping into one universal Truth. To show you what I mean, here are three examples of concepts I've encountered on my own, then found discussed by others.

Concept One:
God as Consciousness
Needing Expression in Matter

~~~~~~~~~~~~~~~~~~~~~~~~~~~

We use many names—God, the Divine, and the Infinite Spirit— to describe what for me is consciousness. It is from this powerful energy that the entire universe has been created. Let us revisit an excerpt from "The Essence of Essence," a channeled piece we looked at earlier that expresses images of how the universe was created and why. In this story, Essence is the Creator and needs to use its energy and vibrations (i.e., consciousness) to create the universe.

Essence wanted to dream.

Essence, being nowhere and everywhere at the same time, wanted to have some visible locations.

Essence wanted the creative challenge of being something, even though it knew in all its wisdom that it would always be what it was in the beginning.

The heart of Essence began to cry and laugh and share all the joys and sorrows.

And as the vibrations began to plump up a bit, they began to spread.

And soon they were calling out to each other

and forming many circles and triangles and squares and hexa-grams

and all other such shapes as it fancied itself.

Receiving the story "The Essence of Essence" was a very moving experience, as I could feel the presence of Essence as One and then experience how the One became many. While the words touched me as they came through, the energy that filled the words is what I remember most about the experience. Essence is sacred, powerful, and in great need of expressing itself in a material way to find out what living is all about.

This passage describes the need of Essence, which we could also name God, to use its own consciousness to create matter. God did not want to remain in an environment where nothing could be learned, so God had to manifest the universe. God had to play the game instead of remaining an energy with no form that could experience itself. God needed to learn from experience. And so the consciousness of God created visible locations, as well as shapes that ultimately became life-forms through which God could experience life.

An Echo from Bernard Haisch

In his book *The God Theory* Bernard Haisch expresses much of the same understanding when he says that he fully expects that science will ultimately prove that consciousness creates matter.

I am also betting that the scientific discoveries in this new millennium will substantiate that the rich inner world of consciousness we all share is more than just a neuro-physiological epiphenomenon. I'm betting that, before too long, we will understand how consciousness, at a fundamental level, creates matter, not vice versa. This view has roots deep in ancient mystical traditions, but is currently heretical to modern science. My wager is this: As science integrates the in-depth knowledge of the physical world accumulated over the past three centuries, it will be channeled into a new and exciting line of inquiry that acknowledges the expanded reality of consciousness as a creative force in the universe and the spiritual creative power embodied in our own minds.

In *The God Theory,* Haisch also presents a quote from Neale Donald Walsch's book *Conversations with God* that echoes the concept that God needed expression in the form of matter. This quote also shows that the consciousness that is God is expanding and dividing itself into separate units of expression: "this and that," just as Essence needs to spread out and have the creative challenge of being something.

Now All That Is knew it was all there was—but this was not enough, for it could only know its magnificence conceptually, not experientially. Yet the experience of itself is that for which it longed, for it wanted to know what it felt like to be so magnificent. Still, this was impossible, because the very term "magnificent" is a relative term. All That Is could not know what it *felt* like to be magnificent unless *that which is not* showed up.

And so All That Is divided Itself—becoming, in one glorious moment, that which is *this* and that which is *that*. For the first time, *this* and *that* existed, quite apart from each other.

An Echo from Gregory Marlowe Teig von Hoffman

One day while I was talking with my eleven-year-old grandson, Greg, he asked about the book I was writing. I told him that I had been involved in a spiritual investigation about God, the creation of the universe, and how the world of spirit communicates with us. Greg then told me he had a story he wanted to share with me. He ran to the nearest computer and wrote:

In the beginning, there was nothing in the universe but gods. Not just one set of gods, mind you; all gods were in the beginning. You see, in the beginning, there were no mortals to separate the gods. All was merry in the hall of gods. This was the only time that Odin and Zeus were friends. But that ended. You see, there is one god that is not recognized for his work, in any time. His name is Master Infinity. Master Infinity was bored. All that happened in the hall of gods was parties, parties, parties. He had hoped that with all of this mighty power, they would do something with it. Now, in the beginning, there was still order, God, Odin, and Zeus were the kings of the hall. Master Infinity was so fed up he just had to complain to them!

"Why is your presence in my hall, Infinity," God bellowed.

"Well, you see, my lords," Master Infinity began. "I have noticed that with all the power we have, the only things we make are party favors, pizza, and beer. Why do we not use this power, to create a greater thing, like alternate intelligent life?"

The lords thought. "Your point is taken, Infinity," Odin echoed. "We *may* indeed create life! Or maybe not."

"So be gone, insignificant one!" Zeus hollered. (As you can see, Zeus and Odin were not nice people.)

"But there must be something I could do to make you think in the other direction," Infinity pondered. "I mean, we cannot be the only ones in the universe. There must be others. And if they won't do it, I will." Master Infinity broke the seal of gods and created the universe without permission. At first, God liked it. Unfortunately, Zeus and Odin became bitter enemies, so Master Infinity was almost banished to hell. Fortunately, he turned his record around by creating an organization that would save worlds. This elite group is called the Infinites. There are only a few from each planet, and while most planets are now aware of them, earth, sadly is not. Something that scientists don't know (is that) the comet that is supposed to wipe out human life already happened. Jac Hcet, son of Greg Hcet, who is the main general of the current Infinites, destroyed it.

Greg's wonderful sense of humor comes through in his story; we see that those in the hall of the gods are only making "party favors, pizza, and beer" when they could be creating "alternate intelligent life." Many of us could make the same statement about people we know in our neighborhood.

Greg's words about Master Infinity's boredom echo passages in "The Essence of Essence." There exists an energy, the most powerful energy, and it has no form in matter. What Greg is calling "power," I am calling "consciousness" or the "Essence of Essence." It is this power, this consciousness, this essence that creates matter—the universe and all living forms.

An Echo from Deepak Chopra

In *Life After Death* (Harmony Books 2006), Deepak Chopra echoes in very plain language: "Other worlds—all worlds, in fact—were formed in consciousness."

It is intriguing to hear other voices ranging from Deepak Chopra to my eleven-year-old grandson, Greg, speak about consciousness, energy, and power. These are minds that are curious about the nature of creation and the evolution of the universe. And each of them, through their own insights and exploration, reach surprisingly similar conclusions: in the beginning there was a consciousness that created our material and human world in order to give expression to its own existence.

Concept Two:
We Must Not Limit Ourselves to Concepts that Traditional Science Can Prove

Before suggesting that science may need an ego adjustment, let us all bow down to science and say thank you a million, trillion, times for all that it has contributed to the world. But please also understand, dear science, that while you are an incredible tool, we simply cannot use you for every single job in the universe that needs to be done, not any more than we could use a hammer to complete every task. While a hammer is the best tool when one wants to nail something to a wall, it is not the best tool for driving across the country; for that, one needs a vehicle!

Having complained a bit to dear science, I do have to add that as a psychic medium, I hope to be as scientific as possible when I give a reading. When I tell you that the spirit of your father is letting me know he was a lawyer when he was alive, I want to be right! However, while I can bring evidence that is verifiable by the client, I also receive messages that cannot be verified. For example, if, in a reading, I tell you that your Aunt Sally had red hair when she was young, you or another family member can verify this information as true or false. However, if you ask me what the spirit of Aunt Sally is doing right now in the world of spirit, there is no way either one of us can verify the answer I receive, as we are not in the world of spirit at this time.

While some psychics and mediums have definite images about what the world of spirit is like, from my point of view, information about what the world of spirit is really like is not verifiable. However, that does not mean that my visions of what is happening in the world of spirit are not correct. If you were able to verify that I was right when I said that your Aunt Sally had red hair, gave birth to three children, and in old age passed because of cancer, then both you and I are more likely to believe that my vision of the spirit of Aunt Sally taking care of the spirits of animals who have just passed over may also be valid. But again, neither one of us can verify any visions I may have about what is happening right now in the world of spirit. It is important for me to bring correct information about the life of Aunt Sally, because that information can be verified, and if true, allows us to be open to messages from Aunt Sally about what is happening in the world of spirit right now.

So as a psychic medium, I utilize and experience two methods of finding Truth: the verifiable, which can be confirmed by other people's knowledge and insights, and the non-verifiable, which can only be accepted as coming from another, more mystical realm. That which can be verified can be subjected to scientific tests; that which is transcendental or mystical is not easily verified.

An Echo from Bernard Haisch

The following words from Bernard Haisch, author of *The God Theory,* bring joy to my heart. Haisch is an astrophysicist, and I am sure he does not offer these words without a lot of thought.

> The problem is that mainstream science has itself become dangerously dogmatic and dismissive of evidence that does not accord with its philosophical beliefs.
>
> In its most extreme form, modern reductionism— the assumption that nothing can be greater than the sum of its parts—precludes any meaningful engagement with a spiritual worldview, because all substantive elements of spirituality are regarded as pure fantasy. Reductionists, who unfortunately represent the majority view of science today, may be comfortable in a limited scientific-spiritual dialogue, but only if the spirituality is reduced (in the true spirit of reductionism!) to moral and ethical codes of conduct. Likewise religious practices, in this dialogue, are interpreted as mere social and cultural events, as if there were no ontological difference between a Saturday night rave and a Sunday morning church service, both merely serving the roles of community rituals.

Haisch goes on to say:

It is acceptable today, even fashionable, to publish scientific papers that propound theories of invisible universes
that may be adjacent to our own in other dimensions.
Some have even postulated universes right on top of our
own, interpenetrating the space we inhabit, supporting
their claims with impressive mathematics that invoke for
example, opposite chirality particles and interactions.
These theories called superstring and M-brane theories
are among the most exciting and prestigious frontiers
of modern physics. They have served as foundations for
many coveted reputations and many successful academic
careers....

    If a religious person talks about transcendental spiri-
tual realities, however, he or she is scoffed at. For some
reason, the eleven-or-twenty-six-dimensional string
worlds of scientific theory are plausible, but the supernatural realms of mysticism are judged to be mere super-
stition.... For some reason, the hypothetical multiverses
and hyperdimensions of modern physics, which remain
purely theoretical, are accepted by science, while the
experimental reports of mystics throughout the ages of
transcendent (i.e., supernatural) realities are dismissed
or ignored. As an astrophysicist, I am partial to observa-
tion: I cannot ignore those experiences. Indeed, it seems
to me that there is better empirical evidence for the existence of God than there is for the many dimensions of
the string theory.

Bravo, Haisch! No one could have articulated those thoughts
better than you did! What Haisch says is so true. Those of us who

are mystically inclined are often thought to be superstitious, making things up or letting our imaginations run wild. Many with a scientific mind-set do not take us seriously. But what a waste my life would be if I did not allow that mystical part of me to operate. While all that I see cannot be proven to be true within scientific method, that does not mean that there is not eternal truth embedded within my visions. I have not said that every vision I have is literally true, but I do feel that there is an energetic truth as the base of each vision. When I communicate with the spirits of those who have passed over, I am not declaring that they are in the same form they were in when they we alive, so, in fact, the visions I am having of them are not literal. Somehow they are able to send images of themselves as they used to be—sometimes mental pictures from three different stages in their life.

And when I receive poems and writings about the creation of the world, I am not declaring that my words are literal, but I am saying that within those words is an energy that is very dynamic and real within its own sphere. I believe that as we merge with deeper and deeper levels of consciousness, we merge with the spheres of light that contain the wisdom of the Divine. And then each one who merges with this truth clothes this wisdom with images and words. But I cannot prove this to a scientist.

If you are mystically inclined, as I am, limiting yourself to insights that can be scientifically proven is not only inappropriate for you, but it would also rob you of all your finest talents. Do I feel badly about reductionist thinkers? Absolutely not, as they prove many theories and invent many things to make our lives better. The world would be in great danger if there were no reductionist thinkers. But we would also be in danger if there were no mystically inclined people. Hopefully, we strike a balance in this life, each of us bringing our own talents to the table of life.

An Echo from Deepak Chopra

Chopra, a medical doctor, does not limit his own views to what traditional science can prove. In *Life After Death* he says, "Science is still burdened by spiritual materialism, the belief that any explanation of God, the soul, or the afterlife is valid only if matter contains the secret. This is like saying we can't understand jazz until we diagram the atoms in Louis Armstrong's trumpet."

Concept Three:
Divine Evolution Is Still in Process,
Exploring Many Potentials

In "The Essence of Essence," it is clear that Essence, who could be called God or the Creator, wants to have visible locations and wants to experience itself. It is also clear that Essence wants to learn from this experience. In order to learn, Essence does not create the universe in which living beings have all the answers. Essence wants that which lives to cope with life and learn from it. By creating an environment of struggle, Essence is manifesting a universe where imagination and creativity are born.

But how can there be a play, if all the players know all the parts, all the time?

It is no learning if One has all the answers at all times.

Ah yes, the answer will remain in the heart of Essence.

But how much more creative and imaginative it would be if all the players did not know all the answers, all the time,

and found themselves in a situation where they could find their pathways home,

and each would find a different pathway,

and Essence would find a hundred thousand, a million, a trillion, a billion souls' answers to finding the way home.

That would be so much more fun

so much more creative

so much more inventive than All Souls having all the answers already.

And so Essence decided that Part of Itself might forget, momentarily, to allow for creativity and imagination to develop to its fullest extent.

Essence is not looking for a standard answer to every question about existence. Essence is looking for a "hundred thousand, a million, a trillion, a billion souls' answers to finding the way home." Only a god who wants to learn and evolve would tolerate the confusion of having to cope with so many answers. Only a god who wants to consider as many possibilities that exist would welcome "so many souls' answers to finding the way home."

An Echo from Bernard Haisch

In *The God Theory*, Haisch speaks to the fact that each individual is part of a complex universe, a speck of potential.

Your conscious being is of the very stuff as God's: your immortal spirit is filtered from God's immortal spirit. Each of us is like one tiny dot of color on a slide of brilliant complexity—and God is the white light of potential out of which we have emerged.

We are all part of God: part of the Essence that has created us. We are complex beings finding many different understandings about life. Our potential is limitless.

An Echo from Ira Progoff

Ira Progoff in *Image of an Oracle* brings us an excerpt from a trance session with internationally famous medium Eileen Garrett. In this excerpt, a spirit speaking through Garrett says:

> The way to see oneself in the midst of it (life), to understand what is happening to the self, that one is here within an ocean of air, bombarded—there is no other word for it—bombarded on all sides, pierced with a thousand arrows of understanding and to put oneself with the magnificence of it. To stand and say "Here I am. This is me. I open myself to the whole vital creative force of life."

A "thousand arrows of understanding" speak to the limitless potential of consciousness, the creative vital force.

So we can see the same concepts echoed many times: Essence finds billions of ways home, Haisch speaks of how each one of us is but a tiny dot on a slide of complexity, and Garrett, in trance, speaks of how we are "pierced with a thousand arrows of understanding." On an intellectual level, where we need words to express our ideas precisely, our perspectives are not exactly alike, but there is a common theme that runs deep within the vibrations that fill all of our words. And the truths that fill the words have greater reality than the words themselves. Our words will always fall short.

As important as words and concepts are to us, perhaps we will find the greatest truth as we sit in the silence and get in touch with the part of each one of us that is a spark of Divine Consciousness. Some of us may then express ourselves in words, while others find another way. When an artist receives the truth, he or she renders it in a glorious statue, an incredible painting, or an exquisite piece of music. When a comic receives a truth, he or she presents it in a manner that has us rolling on the floor with laughter.

As we express ourselves, we will deny each other and we will echo each other. It does not matter, as the truth is so magnificent that it cannot be contained in any of our theories, our concepts, or our artistic expressions. Its value is far beyond what we can describe or prove. And yet each one of us plays an extremely important role in the evolution of this magnificent force, the Essence, because we are all part of it. As we learn, God learns; as God learns, we learn. Evolution depends on the whole of this cosmic experience. Evolution depends on the cosmic connection between all living things, all planets, all dimensions.

Evolution is now.

Chapter 14

All Is Healing

〜〜〜〜

AUTHOR'S NOTE: *This chapter is not intended as a substitute for medical advice. If you have a medical condition, please consult your doctor or healthcare provider.*

IT CANNOT BE REPEATED TOO OFTEN, that healing comes in many forms and one of the most important ways to receive healing is by receiving help from the medical community.

I receive healing not only from the traditional medical community, but from spiritual sources. As I have opened myself to the cosmic realms, I have also felt the presence of healing spirits. My greatest healing has come from the energy that speaks to me and through me, an energy that I have come to call My Guidance or the Energy. The world of spirit has been with me my entire life, sending healing and guidance in different ways. Some special healing experiences stand out as I look back over my life.

The Experience of Healing Spirits at My Feet

〜〜〜〜

In 1988, when I was commuting from Massachusetts to see my husband in New York City, I received an important healing. We had a small but charming apartment, and the view from our living room window was spectacular. At night the city lit up like a Christmas tree, and I would gaze out of this window at the Citicorp building's beautiful display of light. One night I was having trouble sleeping; I decided to move into the living room so that Marlowe, who had to get up and go to work early in the morning, could get some sleep.

I pulled out the sofa bed, tucked myself in, and, after a reasonable amount of tossing and turning, fell asleep. Before I knew it, I was awake again because I felt a presence by my left side. I opened my eyes and what I saw looked like two beings draped in gray capes. These beings did not seem to be male or female. I thought that I must be dreaming, so I pinched myself and moved around the bed to prove to myself that I was awake. Then a most glorious feeling came over me. It was as if healing energy spread throughout my whole body. I can describe what I experienced only as pure bliss. While I did not hear any sound, the beings spoke to me within my mind and said, "Do not worry. We are healing you." Then I felt what I can only describe as a spiritual hand touch my left foot. Before I knew it, the beings were gone, and I was left with a feeling of well-being that I have seldom experienced since then.

The next afternoon, I called several of my friends to tell them what had happened, and my friends heard my story with great excitement.

For a long time I wondered why these visitors had touched my left foot. Did I have a problem? I searched my mind, trying to remember if it had been in my left or right foot that I had torn a ligament in my early twenties. I could not remember. I did know that I had been having pain in my left foot for about five years. If terrestrial beings from the world of spirit were able to send me healing, my left foot would be an obvious place to send it.

At home in Massachusetts, I also had another nighttime visit from these same beings, and again I felt an incredible warm glow after the experience. I was not at all frightened, because I knew that those beings from a realm I knew little about had come to me with the purpose of healing.

These two visitations remain with me today. When I am not feeling well, I visualize these beautiful beings that came to me from somewhere I do not know, with healing and love.

The Time the Virus Lifted Up and Was Gone

I remember once, when I was in my forties, coming down with chills and a sore throat while at a party at a friend's house. I felt a virus entering my body. At this point in my life, I knew about spiritual healing, so I quietly disappeared from the group downstairs and went upstairs to a bedroom. I lay down on the bed, which was piled high with the coats of the guests. I prayed to the healing spirits to remove this virus from me at once. I held my hands over my body and visualized this virus as an energy that was invading my body. I declared to myself that, with the help of the spiritual world, I was going to lift this virus right out of my body. I lifted my hands off of my body and into the air. Suddenly, I felt the virus lift up as if it were an airplane taking off into the skies. It was so real that I could almost feel the shape of it as it left my body. When I got up off the bed, the chill was gone and my throat felt fine. I did not get sick.

This experience has stayed with me, although I have not always been able to repeat it with total success. I do find that when I really believe I can cure myself, I often do. The moment I begin to doubt that healing can take place, I get sick.

I would never stop depending on my living health professionals, as they are also providing healing. However, I believe that the talents of the living health professionals combined with help from the world of spirit give me the best health care I can find.

The Time I Asked for Help and Received

The following are some notes I took after a waking vision and a healing dream. The notes have been edited slightly for clarity. The story begins before I had the waking vision, and it is important to note that the waking vision took place in the middle of the night, after my cat woke me. The dream took place after I went back to sleep.

Last night when I went to sleep, I was upset because a pipe broke in the basement. My basement office flooded, and my husband and I spent at least an hour trying to clean up the place as best we could without the water pump that we would have to rent in the morning. When I finally got to sleep, it was not for long. I woke up in the middle of the night because my cat was crying. He couldn't go into the basement to his litter because of the water.

I was very upset and started thinking about all kinds of terrible things as one can easily do when awakened in the middle of the night. I became quite anxious and distressed. I prayed to my spiritual guidance to please take care of me. I said that I had a lot of work to do with the channeling and that it was too much to have to cope with all these earth problems, such as the flooded basement, as well as the symptoms of my midlife hormonal changes. I began to have a waking vision.

I felt a warm energy spread throughout my body. It was incredible. It was such a striking feeling that I decided to give it a visual form in my mind. So I imagined that above me was a ball of golden energy that was landing about the area of my solar plexus and then spreading throughout my entire body. I started to relax.

All of a sudden I felt a ticklish feeling at the top of my head, right where I would imagine the crown chakra to be. It felt as if someone were making a small incision in the top of my head, yet it only felt like a tickle. I laughed to myself and joked with myself about the fact that the spirits were healing me again as they had done once before. Then I felt a real thud of energy on the outside of my body above where the left ovary is. Then I fell asleep and had the following dream.

I was on a trip with my husband, and he had gone off skiing with his relatives. I had stayed behind in the hotel, and I wasn't having a very good time. I ended up in this party of people who were being healed. Suddenly, I was lying on a table. There were two women in the room who were healers. One of them was standing over me, and she had some strands of thread that she attached to my body about midbody. There were two long strands of thread that joined at the same point on my body. Then she ran around the table, moving those threads so that they formed different kinds of V shapes at different angles as she moved. She was very happy, laughing and having a great time as she performed this act, whatever it was.

When she was finished, she exclaimed that she had removed a cyst from my tailbone area. There was an-other small one on my leg, but it was not a problem, so she did not bother with it. I jumped up and wanted proof that she had done what she had said. She said that she was sorry, but there was no way that she could give me any proof. The last I remember of the dream was that I was a bit confused by the experience.

When I woke, I remembered the other two times in my life that I have had waking dreams in which I have felt the presence of sprits that were healing me. I wondered if I had received a healing once again, but this time from two spirits who appeared to me as women who used some kind of string as they worked.

The Effect of the Waking Vision and the Dream

As I look back on this dream today, I am aware that I asked for help and received it, first in a waking vision and then in a dream. Did healing entities actually remove growths from my body? The healthy skeptic within me says, "I do not think so." But a deeper part of me has an inkling that within the subtle bodies surrounding my physical body there could have been the energetic beginnings of tumors, which had not yet physically manifested, and it was these energetic beginnings that were removed. I feel that as I continue on the spiritual path, I will understand more about how the healing spirits work with each one of us.

I am sure that there are hundreds of spiritual healers around the world who would be able to explain to me, each from his or her own point of view, how it was that this healing took place. But by now, you know how I am: when it comes to spiritual matters, I need to experience things for myself and come to my own conclusions. If the tire on my car goes flat, I am quite happy to turn to someone who knows how to change the tire. If there are mice in my attic, I am extremely eager to have someone else take care of this problem for me. However, when I am trying to understand a spiritual experience, I become a do-it-yourself person. Perhaps this is because I fear getting swept up into the spiritual views of some strange group. But then I have to laugh at myself, realizing that many people will find my experiences to be extremely strange. I am sure some of my companions on the spiritual path have thoughts similar to mine and, like me, feel more protected if they remain independent and avoid becoming overly influenced by others who are exploring spirituality and consciousness.

As I have allowed the memories of the healing visions and dreams to remain with me, my approach to illness has changed. Yes, I go to the doctor whenever I need to, but I also look within, as my health practitioners have taught me to do. Don't get me wrong—it is not that my dentist or doctor has taught me to find deeper states of consciousness. But in order to take care of my teeth and my body, I have to pay attention to myself. As I pay attention, I develop more respect for myself. This feeling of respect causes me to look more deeply within, and I find that I am a spirit connected to a much greater reality than my current cavity or cold. Within this greater reality, I become aware of the spiritual healing available. Knowing that spiritual healing exists, I ask for the healing energies of the universe to heal my current physical or emotional challenge.

One of the important steps on my spiritual path has been to discover Reiki and Spiritualist Healing.

Finding Reiki

It was 1994. I was in Maui for a few weeks to visit my parents. I decided to take a course in Reiki, a Japanese technique for reducing stress. The Reiki practitioner offers the healing by the laying on of hands. Those of us who practice Reiki believe that healing energies are able to flow through our hands to the person receiving the treatment.

I found a wonderful class taught by Brenda Kennerly, who lived on the slope of Haleakala volcano and had an incredible view of the island. I chose her as my Reiki teacher because she is not only a Reiki master, but also an artist. As a musician, I love working with people who are creative! For me, creative energy, healing energy, and spiritual energy come from the same place and, in many ways, are one and the same.

When I first met Brenda, she projected so much love, and her smile was radiant. Over the years, she still has that radiant smile. Recently I asked her, "What are the benefits for you and others when Spirit works through you?"

Brenda replied, "Spirit always helps bring me closer to people. It provides insights about them to me and helps me be more compassionate, less defensive. Spirit helps me see myself and bring me more love for myself. I am very bright, intellectually quick, and sometimes that can get in my way. Spirit opens me up to more than my mind; it opens my heart. And lately I've been feeling more Spirit in my body too, gratefully. So the more I can feel and know that Spirit is in me or I'm part of it—whatever those inadequate words are—it helps me to be real and loving with I myself and with other people too."

Being loving with ourselves and with others is always a challenge, but this challenge is ultimately what healing is all about!

I found Brenda to be an incredible Reiki instructor, and she has been an exciting person to stay in touch with over the years. Here is a story about an experience I had as a result of attending her class.

One day, we left class with an assignment: we were to practice giving a Reiki treatment to another person. I called my friend Hazel, who, with her husband, Paul, owned and operated Maui's most well-known hamburger joint, Bullocks. People all over the world who have traveled to Maui and driven up the highway to Haleakala Crater remember Bullocks for its famous "moon burger." This place, now closed, had been my dad's hangout for years, and I had become close friends with Paul and Hazel Elkins.

I asked Hazel if I could practice my Reiki treatment on her, and she said, "Sure, come on down to the shop." As Hazel and I sat down in one of the booths, I asked if she had any aches and pains. Hazel, at that time in her mid-eighties, replied as usual that she was fine and had *no* aches and pains. However, she said that she was curious to see if I could do anything with her pinky finger. I looked at the pinky of her right hand, and sure enough, the bottom part of it was turned at an odd angle. Hazel said that she had arthritis in that finger, plus she had injured it. That lower section of her finger had been turned in the wrong direction for many years. She simply could not straighten it.

I held her pinky finger in my hands and prepared my mind to receive the healing energies that would then flow through my hands to Hazel. Once the treatment began, I held her finger for about five minutes, and as I did so, both my hands and Hazel's finger got quite hot. When I let go of her finger, I reached over to see if I could straighten it. It was hard to believe, but I was able to do so. Hazel nearly fell off her chair.

"This can't be happening," I cried out.

Hazel said in her matter-of-fact voice: "Well, it is happening, honey, as my finger is straight!"

I tried to find every explanation I could to disprove what had just happened. I decided that maybe her finger had been straighter than I had thought in the first place. I was upset with myself for not having measured the angle of her finger before and after the Reiki treatment. I was determined to conduct the next treatment like a real experiment.

The next day I called Hazel and asked her how her finger was. Well, it was bent again, but not as much as before the healing session. I said, "I'll be right over." This time I arrived with a ruler and paper and pencil. Before I started the healing session, I traced Hazel's right hand so that I could see exactly how far her finger was bent. Then I did the healing session, and, lo and behold, she could straighten it again. When I finished, I drew a second picture of her right hand, and, comparing the two pictures, it was clear that her finger was bent before the session and straight after the session. Hazel and I sat and stared at each other. We did not know what to say.

Although I asked Hazel if I could work on her hand every day for a couple of weeks to see if we could get her finger to remain flexible, she became too busy for the sessions. I think she was bewildered and a touch frightened. I was disappointed that I did not get to give her any more Reiki treatments, but I was extremely grateful to have had this experience and to see that Reiki, which is a spiritual form of healing, can work.

Finding Spiritualist Healing

In the early nineties I started attending a Spiritualist church regularly. In a standard Sunday service, part of the hour and a half is dedicated to spiritual healing. The minister invites members of the church who have been trained as healers to come up toward the front of the church and to stand behind the chairs that have been set up to be used in the healing portion of the service. The minister lets the congregation know that the healers are not healing those who will sit in the chairs, but that they are channeling the healing energy of God. It is explained that the healers will place their hands on the head, neck, shoulders, and upper back only. Some Spiritualist ministers also make it clear that spiritual healing works hand in hand with the medical community and that Spiritualist healers never diagnose or offer advice on medical treatment. Once the minister has finished the explanation to the congregation, members of the congregation are invited to come forward and sit in a healing chair. They are instructed to focus on healing for themselves, for another person, or for an issue that is going on in the world.

When I first started sitting in a healing chair during church services, I did not know what I would experience. I found that every time I sat in a healing chair I felt better. And when I had been a Spiritualist long enough to be trained as a healer, I found that standing behind the chair and acting as a channel for the healing energies was extremely powerful.

When I am a channel for the healing energies of the world of spirit, it does not matter to me whether I call it a Reiki treatment or Spiritualist Healing. The label is unimportant. What is important is the realization that those of us who are able to become clear channels for healing can receive the healing energies through our hands. Many forms of spiritual healing are available for all of us to learn and practice.

Why do some people heal physically and some don't? This question is one that all of us have asked. It ranks right up there with questions such as why does one person get sick and another lives a healthy life until age ninety? Why do some people die when they are children? Why are there wars? Why do people suffer so much pain during their lifetimes? Science, religion, philosophy, psychology, and, I am sure, a host of other "ologies" try to answer these deep questions.

In one of the channeling sessions of the Sitting Project, we discussed healing with My Guidance. Ron, a Spiritualist who has worked for the credential of "commissioned healer" with the American Federation of Spiritualist Churchs, asked about the role of the spiritual healer. My Guidance replied:

> The healer works with the person in need. The energy that comes through the healer simply announces to the ones receiving the healing that healing is available. But it is the soul receiving the healing that makes the decision as to what form the healing is going

to take. The soul receiving the healing knows if it is time to go back home to eternal life or whether it is time to recover from the symptoms. But all the healer is doing is providing an environment and a setting so that the energy can flow through and say that healing is available. But it is the soul of the individual that decides how that healing is to go and how it will manifest.

From our point of view, too much emphasis has been put on the healer and the energy coming through the healer that is going to somehow do something to the one in need. But that is not how, from our energetic perspective—that is not what happens. Again, the healer creates an environment, and in a sense it is like knocking on the door and saying, "Hello, healing is at the door."

Ron asked, "What you say suggests there could be a disparity between what the soul feels is appropriate in respect to a healing situation and what the incarnate mind wants." My Guidance responded:

The soul knows whether it is time to go home to the eternal life of the spirit or it is time to heal from the symptoms that are present at the moment. Whatever is in the mind of the healer or in the mind of the individual with the symptoms is of little consequence. Because that is all on a level of the personality and the soul, which is connected to the Divine Energy, is in a different realm: Very difficult to put this into language.

Even though I am in a deep altered state of consciousness when I channel and bring through the messages, there is a part of my mind that is aware of what is being said. I was not at all happy when My Guidance made the previous statement. It is very hard for me to accept that it is always the soul's decision when there is an automobile accident and a family is instantly killed. I cannot believe that when a small child dies, it is because the soul has decided it is time to go home.

However much I agree or disagree with the words, it is my job as a channel to faithfully bring them through. And, in fact, once in a deep state, I no longer have a lot of control over the words I speak. I feel like my Greater Self is translating into statements the energy that comes from a broader perspective. The messages that come through are more than I, the personality of Carole Lynne, can conceive of.

As much respect as I have come to have for the words that flow through me, if I disagree, I do not take those words on board as the absolute truth. In fact, when the spirit of a young child comes through in a reading to speak with my client, who is the child's mother, I stick to my own ideas rather than repeating the words of My Guidance. The mother may ask me at the end of the session why her child died or may ask if this death was meant to be. I always respond, "There are many people who feel that there is a destined time for each one of us to leave our bodies and return home to the world of spirit, but I am not of that belief. I cannot believe that this child was meant to die. I believe that in our world we have accidents; there are real diseases, and there is a real thing called tragedy. Some individuals die prematurely or, as we often say, 'before their time.' I cannot find any other explanation for your child's death than tragedy." And when I say that to a sobbing mother or father, I sincerely mean it.

There was, however, a reading, in which the spirit of a child came through and told us specifically that he had made the decision to return home, and it was the right decision. In this case, I had to bring the message that I received from the child in spirit. I believed the spirit of this child, and it felt right to bring this message to the parents.

Some parents believe that the soul knows when it is time to go home, while others believe their child's death was not planned or part of any spiritual destiny. I never try to persuade anyone to accept my beliefs, because these questions about when we die are extremely difficult to answer and the conclusions we each come to cannot be verified. Our conclusions are also highly personal. Why some of us heal from accidents and illness and some of us do not is a controversial question, and we may not all agree as we try to find answers. Perhaps this question is one of the mysteries of life and death.

Be Like Hazel, the Eternal Healer

Today, as I look back on the many healing experiences I have had, I feel taken care of by the world of spirit. But I know many of us yearn for a security that does not exist. We would all like to know that we can be cured of any illness by our doctors and with the help of the energy that is channeled by spiritual healers; however, there is no kind of insurance that will guarantee our continued physical health. On the other hand, whether we possess physical health or not, there is an assurance that we can heal spiritually. If we are ill, we must try to remember that it is only the physical body that is ill. The spirit within each one of us can be healthy at all times if we allow ourselves to open up to the wisdom of our Greater Selves.

As I write these words, I am in good health, and so I realize that it is easier for me to offer these words than it is to follow their truth. I am fortunate to have known a number of people who received spiritual healing throughout their lives. They did not announce it or label the experience, but one could tell by their attitudes that they received spiritual healing. For instance, Hazel, the lady who allowed me to do the Reiki treatments on her finger, is one of those positive people. She lived to be ninety-four years old and had an incredible attitude toward life. I know Hazel had pain, and I know she had illness. But as far as Hazel was concerned, she was always healthy. You could not tell Hazel she was sick, or she would glare at you. When she had her final heart attack and was refusing to go to the hospital, perhaps it was because Hazel's soul knew it was time to go home to the eternal life she knew was waiting for her.

Hazel Elkins was spiritual healing living in a human body. Healing energies exuded from her. Her attitude, her warmth, and her smile healed every person who sat down in her café to order a cup of coffee and a moon burger. No wonder Bullocks was always crowded; it was a spiritual temple for those who sat there and received day after day.

As I get older and my physical body starts to fall apart to let me know that it has had enough of this life, I hope I can remember Hazel's strength and healing attitude. I hope I can remember that healing is always available. Hazel knew that and received healing all her life. And I guess I am fortunate that Hazel was a lot older than I, because it means that the spirit of Hazel will be there to help me heal when I move on.

In the religion of Spiritualism, we believe and prove through our demonstrations of spirit communication that our spirits live on when our physical lives on earth are over. Knowing that our consciousness survives the death of the physical body has helped many to become less afraid of facing the end of physical existence. Here are some inspirational words by Rev. Mary Di Giovanni, pastor of the Greater Boston Church of Spiritualism:

> At no time do I feel more alive than when I am linked with loved ones from Spirit. The life force that exists within their vibration is far greater than the life force that we experience in our lives on earth. As a sensing

being, I have found that we, our essence as it is experienced on earth, are heavy and dense; those in Spirit are light and vibrant. This experience of sensing and feeling those on the spirit side of life has eliminated all fear of death and helped me to realize that death is a doorway that we will all walk through when we are ready to continue to progress along our spiritual journey. But I have also learned that we do not have to walk through that door to progress spiritually—that is something that we are participating in every moment of every day. When our learning here is finished and we have evolved as much as we can here on earth, our plan accomplished, then we will be called home to continue.

Hazel was never a Spiritualist, but she knew that life was continuous. Her spiritual knowledge came naturally to her.

Chapter 15

Love Is the Answer to the Question Living Brings

~~~~~~~~~~~~~~~~~~~~~~~~~~~~~~~~~~~~

IT WAS IN THE SEVENTIES, and I was living in Mill Valley, California. I was writing so many songs I did not know what to do with them. It was great fun to go out a couple nights a week and sing at places like the Fondue Pot, Marin Joe's Restaurant, and many other bars and restaurants in Marin County. I'd sing my songs about love and romance. I'd sing my songs about the feminist revolution and mix in a few jazz songs Ella Fitzgerald had made popular, followed by a song by the Eagles. I was acoustic, and I was eclectic! Driving across the Golden Gate Bridge in my red VW bus to do gigs in San Francisco is one of my fondest memories. Sometimes the wind on the bridge would be so fierce it seemed like my bus would topple over. I guess the heavy amplifiers I had in the back of the bus kept me grounded. I was not really afraid. I was thirty-five years old, and the world was mine. Nothing could happen to me.

One day, when I was writing a song, I felt strange, as if I were being lifted into another reality where the song was simply there, and I did not need to write it. All I had to do was take down the words and quickly record the song before I forgot the melody. Perhaps I was entering that land somewhere over the rainbow.

A line came to me that day that I have never forgotten: "Love is the answer to the question living brings."

Living does bring question after question: What shall I do with my life? What shall I study? How can I get along with my parents? How I can get along with my spouse? How can I cope with this illness? What do I want to do before my life is over? And so on.

Life is also full of fear-filled questions: What shall I do if they do not like me? Why am I not smart enough, pretty enough, thin enough, rich enough? Why don't I make as much money as my friends? Why doesn't my family understand me? What will happen if the economy collapses, if a war breaks out? And so on.

If I had a dollar for every fearful thought I have had that has not come true, I would be a billionaire by now. Of course, like most people, I have had hard times, but usually the most difficult things that have happened have not been the things I have feared. All the fear I have experienced has been a huge waste of time and precious energy. I wish I could have realized this when I was younger, but perhaps one does not get to know this truth until later on in life.

Fear is not the answer. Worry is not the answer. Love is the answer.

Whatever the problems, whatever the worry, accept it with love, and you will find a solution. Whatever happens, know that you are spirit and that you have been born into this world in love, and you will leave this world in love.

Perhaps learning that life is eternal and that our consciousness survives the death of the physical body has changed my perspective. I give thanks to everyone who has ever invited me to do a reading for them and allowed me to be part of the sacred communication from their loved ones who have passed over. Each time I do a reading, I learn once again that we are eternal spirits. I do not think I will ever become blasé about this experience.

The love that pours through from those who have passed over is astounding.

Learning in my channeling sessions that my Greater Self is able to merge with the cosmos to bring in messages about the nature of cosmic reality has changed me a bit, to say the least. The transcripts of the sessions can sound fantastic to me when I am in my everyday state of mind—my go-to-the-grocery-store state of consciousness. However fantastic the messages sound, I am truly inspired by the words that come through. I have realized that it is my Greater Self that connects with this cosmic energy, decodes it, and translates it into words. The fact that it is not an individual spirit guide bringing me the messages in no way detracts from the sacred quality of the experience. The cosmos is all the more sacred to me because I know that it is beyond words and images. And the cosmic connection is not mine. Any person who is willing and able to open up to the Greater Self can receive guidance and healing. Each one of us is a spark of the Divine, and no one has a monopoly on Divine Knowledge.

No One Has a Monopoly on Divine Energy or Truth

No one can regulate how Divine Energy expresses itself through different individuals. The Divine speaks through each one of us through our deeper states of consciousness. There is a spark within each one of us that is part of Divine Consciousness; it is this part that receives the message and brings it forth. If two people receive messages, those messages will never come through with the same words. The Divine speaks to us, and we each bring through the wisdom in our own way. This principle explains why there are so many religions built on different revelations by different men and women who feel they have connected with the Divine. Some will say that they have received revelations from God, while others will say that they are communicating with Divine Consciousness or with an angel. The names we use for the Divine are different and the words that come through in our revelations are different because ultimately the Divine source from which we come and of which we are part is beyond words. The Divine is the Divine no matter how we perceive it.

Spirit speaks to us in many ways—in dreams, in revelations, in personal experiences, in messages from loved ones who have passed over, in advice given by those who live in the world of spirit and guide us in our daily lives. All is Spirit. Whatever the name, the light is the same.

If there is any one answer to be found, it is love. Finding love is a journey that we each take, and we do not ride on the same vehicle. Perhaps you find love on a trip across the country on a motorcycle. Perhaps you find love playing your viola in an orchestra or building houses in many countries in the world. It is not for me to say how you can find love or how you will find love. But I will say that love is the answer. I have found love through my family and my close friends. I have found love through music and art. And I have found love through the cosmic connection to those in the world of spirit.

Love brings peace. Love brings courage. Love is the answer to the question living brings.

The following session took place on April 21, 1992, one of my early years of channeling. I was going to use the words that came through as the basis for a meditation in a seminar, but never got around to it. The other day I found them and realized that they are for you.

If you want to connect with your own spirit, with the spirits of your loved ones, and with the spirits of those who have passed on, open up to the pool of ecstasy that is waiting for you.

CAROLE LYNNE IN HER OWN VOICE: This morning I am having many thoughts go through my mind. It is almost hard to imagine that I can bring through guidance from another sphere of reality, and my mind wanders again to wondering what this energy is that comes through me. How am I connected to it?

(I count down from ten to one, bringing myself into a deeper state of consciousness.)

MY GUIDANCE: The vision you see is of kittens romping and playing in a very joyful way. And a puppy dog comes over and licks them. You see the birds flying outside.

Nature is there for you if you will but open up to it and let the glories of nature and the universe ring through your body and your soul.

Fear destroys the resonance and keeps you from experiencing life on earth to its fullest.

Allow yourself the creativity of your imagination, and many things will flow as you have seen they have started doing already.

Coincidences and synchronicities will abound in this time period if you will but open up and believe.

Let the magic carry you the way that you let it carry you this morning when you fixed your tape recorder. Was it the banging on the side of the tape recorder that fixed it, or was it your belief that somehow you could be in resonance with the energy of that tape recorder and it would work again?

You believed it, and it worked. Was it a miracle? No, it was the interchange of energies.

And you can have this effect on many things and people around you if you will but believe it.

Ah, belief! Belief is the energy that changes matter.

"What does it matter" is an expression you use. What does it? Matter. You do it.

A cloud floats by, and it may contain rain. It may hide the sun. It may move over and let the sun's radiance reach you.

All of it is good.

Do not worry or spend a great deal of time trying to control the weather.

I wonder whether it will be a good day today—weather it will be a good day.

CAROLE LYNNE IN HER OWN VOICE: My vision takes me into a cave now—into what looked like it was going to be a very dark cave. But as I enter the cave, the energy from my body starts to light it up.

And as the energy from my body touches the dark walls, it begins to become alive with crystals.

And the walls hold many spirits and vibrations in the crystals.

And now they are beginning to speak to me.

I feel the energy from all the spirits in the side of this cave. The spirits are telling us:

"There is a pool of ecstasy waiting for those who would care to enter it.

"There is a pool of ecstasy waiting for those who would cross the fine line between diligence, responsibility, and ecstasy.

"There is a pool of ecstasy waiting for those who would allow themselves to meet their true spiritual selves, and allow themselves to suffer both the pain and anguish which that meeting brings, along with the joy and hope and faith that such a meeting enriches.

"What are the things in our lives that keep us from this pool of ecstasy, this spiritual place in ourselves that allows us to be in contact with God, with nature, with that which makes us really happy?

"There is a pool of ecstasy waiting for those of us who are brave enough to shed the rules that we have lived by and to look instead for a way to live in harmony with our inner selves.

"But, oh, what will this one think?

"And what will that one think?

"And what will this one say?

"And what will that one do,

"if I do not follow the line that has been written by others?

"Will they think I am unsuccessful?

"Will they think I am lazy?

"Will they think I am not a good citizen?

"Oh dear, what will they think of me,

"if I do not follow the line that they have written?

"Or is it 'they'?

"Can I put the blame on 'they'?

"Perhaps it is 'I' that have written such a line,

"and that when I check it out with 'them,'

"'they' would not have me live such a rigid life after all.

"And so why do I write myself into this story that is like writing myself into a prison with inescapable walls with schedules so tight that I can hardly breathe?

"Why do I write myself into this corner where there is no light?

"And, oh, the glory and the wondrous sensation when I allow myself to be in the true flow of my life instead of writing myself into that tight corner!

"And I breathe, and I let out a sigh that says, 'I am happy. I am in the flow of my life as it should be.'

"Oh, but if I could allow myself to be in that flow more often.

"There is a pool of ecstasy waiting for those who would find the true spirituality within their hearts.

"Words from others can prompt it.

"Lessons from others can help it.

"But the true flow is beyond words.

"And one must find it within themselves.

"There is a pool of ecstasy waiting for those who would dare to confront themselves and enter that pool."

Allow yourself to be in the flow of your life—free to be with yourself, free to be with your loved ones, and free to be aware of the spirit within you that connects with the world of spirit. This is the pool of ecstasy there for all of us.

Chapter 16

Love in Action to Create a Better World

~~~~~~~~~~~~~~~~~

Spirit has spoken to me in many ways: dreams, waking visions, and messages I receive when in an expanded and deeper state of consciousness. The spirits of your loved ones and mine have also spoken to me and continue to speak to me as they prove again and again that life is continuous. My concept of reality has widened and changed.

In my spiritual journey I have learned we are all One. I realize that many spiritual teachers, poets, and songwriters have made this statement. Perhaps the reason this truth has been stated so many times is because this statement is the ultimate truth. If the world of science has the opportunity to prove that there is a Divine Consciousness (which many call God), it will be because it has been concluded that all that exists is made out of the same thing: consciousness.

In my individual, narrow conscious state, I cannot know the things that I know when I access my Greater Self, that part of me that is able to make the cosmic connection with the Divine. I cannot receive the wisdom when I am parking my car, doing the laundry, and fighting with my computer when there are technical problems. I do not see the spheres of light that contain the truth when I am taking care of everyday business. In that state, I do things like get mad at my husband, accidently drop a book on my friend's foot, and lock the keys inside my car.

On the personality level, like most of us, I want what I want. But as I allow myself to explore the wider realms of consciousness, I begin to see past my own nose, past my own personal desires, and I become more aware of our world and of the greater universe. As I contemplate our world, realizing that we are all One, it is clear that I share in the responsibility for our world. It is my fault that wars continue, the earth is polluted, and people take illegal drugs. It is my fault that people get drunk and abuse each other. Why? Because I am a tiny spark of Divine Consciousness, as is every other human being on this earth. Everything that happens on this planet and within the universe influences what is the whole of who we are. Every action I take creates a ripple in the whole of who we are. Therefore, I am responsible.

Coping with Conflicting Ideas

I spent so much time during the seventies and eighties learning to focus on myself and to stop feeling so responsible for the actions of others. Now I am saying that I am responsible for the actions of the whole world! How am I to cope with these conflicting ideas?

My Guidance brings me the answer to that question in the story "The Essence of Essence": "You will remember, and then you will feel the love that Essence brings you. And that love will flow from you to others on your planet." If I am part of the problems that have been created in our world, it follows that I must become part of the solutions.

In my everyday state of mind, I cry, "I am an individual and I am not responsible for the actions of others." But the cosmic connection within me responds by transporting me to a realm where I know I am. As I let go and travel to the deeper state, these words come to me:

> As I open up to wider states of consciousness and remember that I am a spark of the Essence of Divine Consciousness, I know we are all One. Knowing that I am part of One, I will live my life differently than before and in doing so serve as a model or teacher for others. Of course, I cannot control the actions of another individual, and on an individual level I am not responsible for the lives of other individuals. But on a deeper level, that realm in which we are all One, I am doing my part by changing my values. As I change my values, I am more loving to myself and to the world.

As each one of us realizes we are part of the whole, light becomes available to us. This light cannot be described accurately. You can read a million words about this light, and hundreds of people can lecture to you about it, but you can only experience it for yourself. No one can give it to you. But once you have opened to it and received it, the light that has become part of your vibrational pattern will shine and attract others. You will change your actions and influence others. You will make better choices, and your choices will speak louder than words!

For example, Al Gore and those who worked with him made a great choice by creating the film *An Inconvenient Truth.* The research and lectures on our current environmental crisis influenced me. While some people may question whether this documentary is 100 percent accurate, the basic conclusion remains the same: we need to change the way we consume energy. The climate is changing, and regardless of how it happened and whether it is our fault or part of a natural earth cycle, we still need to change the way we consume energy. Al Gore's light has shined on me, and he has become a model for others. Let us, as

Al Gore has, try to influence others to take actions that are helpful to our world.

As a result of watching *An Inconvenient Truth,* my husband and
I are now trying to conserve energy by turning off all lights and
other electrical equipment in the house when they are not in
use. We have, during some months, reduced our electricity bill
by almost 50 percent. We are also trying to make sure that we
eat the food in our house before buying more food. The things
that we are doing are not only helping the world, but also saving
us money—money that we now have to buy a new hybrid car,
which allows us to consume less gasoline. The hybrid car does
not have the most comfortable seat and there are other cars I
would rather have. But the light that has shined within me speaks
to me now more of the time—sometimes even when I am in my
everyday, go-to-the-grocery-store-state of consciousness—and
says, "Carole, make a choice for the world and give up some of
your personal preferences."

I have a long way to go in terms of making better choices
for the world. I do not know that I am willing to suffer through
a hot and humid night without the use of my air conditioner, for
instance. But I am at the point where I am considering turning it
off on as many days as I can tolerate the heat of the New England
summer. The fact that this thought is entering my mind on a conscious level tells me that I am moving toward making a change
in my behavior.

How Can We Make Changes?

Before we will change our behavior, we have to change our
minds. We have to change our minds about what is important. If
we want to make substantial changes in our lifestyles, we have to

explore our deeper states of consciousness. There are thousands of environmental books and many websites that tell us the practical ways to make lifestyle changes. With this information in hand, we can make lists of things to do. But these lists will gather dust on our kitchen counters until we change from within. It is by spiritual growth that we will move forward. As we realize we are all One, we will change our behavior.

I am not asking you to join any particular religion or to join a spiritual or environmental group. If you want to change, you need to look within. Take time to be with yourself. Talk to the spirit within. And remember that none of us needs drugs or alcohol to explore deeper states of consciousness. (With all due respect to ancient cultures that may have used drugs as part of their spiritual ceremonies, time marches on, and we have learned that we do not need mind-altering substances to be part of our spiritual explorations.)

What we do need is a commitment to explore the deeper spiritual realms so that our expanding state of awareness will move us to make the difficult choices that are necessary in order to protect ourselves and our home: the earth. However, there is no point in sitting and contemplating our navels or climbing to the top of the mountain if it is not going to result in better choices. Let us ask ourselves if any choice we are about to make is kind or unkind, helpful or destructive.

It is not easy to change. If you feel inclined, find a spiritual mentor or friend to talk with about your spiritual explorations. Sometimes we need support as we change.

Rev. Irene Harding, a Spiritualist minister speaks to us about spiritual unfoldment:

Our earth life is many times perceived as a journey that is all about survival. When we come to the realization that our time in the physical involves our spiritual evolution, we are then on the pathway of claiming our true identity. Spiritual unfoldment begins when we do not live from the external, but from the internal, where we house our true spiritual essence. This knowledge leads us to the power to master the long, subtle process of unfolding our spiritual potential.

As we focus on the internal, we will realize we are all One. Only then will we make substantial changes. Only then will we manifest our power and use that power for the good of the One. As our thoughts become less self-centered, our actions will change. We will put our personal preferences aside in order to live a better life for the One. It is ironic, but it is in raising our consciousness that we will ultimately protect our physical survival on this planet.

You may remember the line by Jimi Hendrix: "When the power of love overcomes the love of power, the world will know peace."

Our mothers taught us that actions speak louder than words. Right now our actions say that we believe that war is the way to settle differences. Our actions say that we believe that there is not enough food in the world for everyone. We have all heard by now the rational reasons why we have war, poverty, and pollution. We have all heard the intellectual statements about why these conditions are so hard to change. With our logical minds, we can all follow, understand, and even come away with a stoic acceptance of the harsh realities of human life. But the truth is, our logic is failing us. We are not finding the love that is the answer to our world crisis. We have to take a leap in our world consciousness in order to find solutions that do not destroy us. As long as we believe in the actions we are now taking, the world will continue to develop more wars, more poverty, and more pollution.

I do not profess to be a politician, historian, or scholar. There are great minds that can argue me right under the table, as I cannot keep up with all these intellectual arguments about the ways of the world. My common sense, my intuition, and my spiritual experiences have guided me. I believe that our world will not change until there are enough people who find our current behaviors to be irrational and destructive. If one person at a time opens to the Greater Self within, eventually war, poverty, and pollution will be unthinkable. There will always be wars until the consciousness of the whole world has risen to a point where we cannot tolerate war as a way of settling our differences. There will always be poverty until we have risen to a point where we cannot tolerate poverty. There will always be pollution until we cannot imagine harming our beautiful world.

As I write these words, I suffer inside as I know there is so much more I could be doing to help the world. Yes, I donate to worthy causes and do my volunteer work, but there is always more that I could be doing. I am certain many of you can relate to this feeling. The changing of my habits is a work in progress. I am not certain about how many changes I can make and how quickly I can make these changes. Like you, I will do the best I can. I lift up my foot and prepare myself to take another step on the spiritual path in order to change my behaviors. It is a difficult journey, and I pray for patience.

The Spiritual Path to Change

For a long time I have yearned to share the story of my spiritual experiences, and I appreciate that you have received my story. My story is about connection—cosmic connection. My Greater Self has merged with an energy that is intelligent, forceful, and the essence of the creative force. Perhaps as I continue on the spiritual path, the personality-level Carole Lynne will start to catch up with my Greater Self. This energy is within each one of us if we will only open to it. This creative force picks up information and drops it off in other parts of the universe. This energy learns from us and teaches us. It is the essence of the forces of evolution. Let us listen to this creative force within; let us find better solutions for ourselves and for our world.

If you are not already in touch with the Greater Self within, your connection to the Divine, I pray that you get in touch with it. I do not care how you personify what is the ultimate. What I do care about is that each one of us makes the cosmic connection and gets in touch with this universal force, so that we are influenced for the greater good of the world and no longer do things like leave garbage on the beach or do mean things to one another.

On the spiritual path I still encounter many uncertainties. By no means do I have it all figured out. In fact, I feel as if I am still at the beginning of the path of spiritual discovery. But there is one thing I am certain about: the more I am in touch with my Greater Self, the more I will receive the light. As I receive the light, I will change. When I started focusing on spiritual development in 1987, my conscious mind knew a lot less than it knows today. As I continue to concentrate on spiritual development, my Greater Self has more impact on the everyday Carole Lynne.

What about you? What are you going to do to be more helpful to yourself, to our world, and to our universe?

I have shared my experience with you, which is my attempt to be helpful. I hope that you are motivated to listen to yourself—to go within and find the light. And, of course, I understand that your conclusions on the spiritual path may be different than mine.

But before I conclude this important step on my path, I ask you to consider one thing: there is a place where you and I meet, a place deep within the wider consciousness of existence, where it would be hard for us to know the difference between you and me. I know that you and I meet in this place regularly, and within this realm "you and I" are not "you and I." We are all One. I will meet you within that Oneness.

And perhaps I will even meet you on the material level, as human beings who are living out our lives. If you do meet me on this level, remember that I will most likely be in my everyday go-to-the-grocery-store state of consciousness, so do not step on my foot or accidently bang your grocery cart into mine. I may snap at you, and you may frown at me. And then we will laugh at each other. After all, we are human, aren't we?

I leave you to explore your own consciousness—or rather, "We leave us to explore our own consciousness." Or, as My Guidance would impart, "One explores consciousness."

Resources

~~~~~~

American Federation of Spiritualist
Churches
P.O. Box 1840
Sagamore Beach, MA 02562
United States
www.afschurches.com

Arthur Findlay College
Stansted Hall
Stansted CM24 8UD
England
www.arthurfindlaycollege.org

Best Psychic Mediums
www.bestpsychicmediums.com

Babies Need Food Foundation
The Rani Roberts Memorial
Corporation
87 Common Street
Watertown, MA 02472
United States
www.babiesneedfood.org

National Spiritualist Association of
Churches
13 Cottage Row
P.O. Box 217
Lily Dale, NY 14752
United States
www.nsac.org

Spiritualist National Union
SNU Registered Office
Redwoods, Stansted Hall
Stansted CM24 8UD
England
www.snu.org.uk

Sri Aurobindo Society
Pondicherry, India
Email: info@sriaurobindosociety.org.in
www.sriaurobindosociety.org.in

Acknowledgments

~~~~~~~~~~~~~

I GIVE GREAT THANKS to the three health practitioners to whom I have dedicated this book: Dr. Jeanne Hubbuch, my physician; Dr. Robert Gensler, my chiropractor; and Dr. Paul Duffell, my dentist. One might wonder why a psychic medium and channel is dedicating a book to her health practitioners: these three professionals have served me for over twenty-five years, taught me to focus on taking care of myself, and encouraged me to lead a balanced life. Without this balance, I do not think I would be able to lead the life of a psychic medium, author, musician, and family member. I am often going in many directions at once. While my doctors are not representing or endorsing my spiritual explorations, the help they have given me and continue to give me allows me to have the energy to write books, travel to numerous countries in the world, and provide readings and seminars for many people.

I would like to thank my Weiser Books publisher Jan Johnson, who has taken an active role in the development of the *Cosmic Connection* manuscript. Her insights and comments have helped me to shape years of spiritual experiences into a book that can help others understand their own experiences in order to live more successful lives and to develop into people who can help our troubled world. I can be shy at times, and Jan has encouraged me to share more fully with my readers. I cannot thank her enough.

My thanks are also extended to many others at Weiser Books, including Michael Kerber and Bonni Hamilton for their help in putting *Cosmic Connection* out into the world.

I would like to thank Ron Monroe and Bob Blake for their commitment to what we named the Sitting Project, founded in 2004. They have given their time to our project for several years and have made it possible for me to allow myself to go into a deeper altered state of consciousness than I would when sitting in meditation by myself during the years 1987 through 2004. As they have sat with me during my more recent sessions, they have protected me by making sure that I take enough time going into and coming out of what I feel is a light trance state. With their support, I have been able to bring through many inspired dialogues that I'm sharing with you in *Cosmic Connection*—words that reflect on the nature of the universe and point us in the direction of what we need to do in order to lead better individual lives and create a better world where we are all one, helping each other.

My appreciation goes to the guests who attended Sitting Project sessions: from England, Minister Brenda Lawrence and Minister Nora Shaw, and from the United States, Rev. Simeon Stefanidakis. Our guests brought us insights about the way we conducted our sessions, as well as asking challenging questions.

Grateful thanks goes to my Spiritualist teachers and colleagues from whom I have learned so much. Special thanks go to Rev. Irene Harding and Rev. Mary DiGiovanni from the American Federation of Spiritualist Churches for the messages they included in the conclusion of the book. While I have shared much with my friends in Spiritualism, I state emphatically that in this book I am representing myself and presenting stories of my own experiences. In no way am I representing any Spiritualist other than myself, nor am I representing any of the Spiritualist organizations.

My good friends in India have been extremely helpful. I would like to thank Vijay Poddar at the Sri Aurobindo Ashram in Pondicherry for his guidance during the past few years as I have been writing this book, which includes my reactions to visiting the Sri Aurobindo Ashram and reading many books by Sri Aurobindo and the Mother. He has faithfully read the chapter on Sri Aurobindo and the Mother and edited my comments as needed. It is my hope that, with Vijay's help, I have been able to state my views about the writings of Sri Aurobindo and the Mother in a manner that shows respect to all those who study their teachings. I would also like to thank Gita Patel for her attention to me during my visits to the Ashram. Her guidance and enthusiasm for my writing have been appreciated.

My thanks go to Bob Olson, founder of *BestPsychicMediums. com* and *Ofspirit.com,* for his continued support and frequent consultation with me on all my projects. I feel extremely fortunate to have the attention of such a smart and creative person. Bob fully understands my spiritual work and helps me to share my work in a way that is dignified and sacred. Bob presents psychic mediums in a respectful manner, and I am forever grateful to him.

I wish to extend my thanks to John Roberts for the part he played in encouraging me to share my spiritual stories. I met John, a retired Seventh Day Adventist minister from India, when my son was making plans to marry his daughter, Anita. Over the past ten years, John and I have had many conversations. Although we come from entirely different theological backgrounds—he is a Seventh Day Adventist and I am a Spiritualist—we see eye to eye on many spiritual topics. I confided to John that I was afraid of sharing my spiritual visions with the general public, as people are so quick to call those who share their visions "impostors." But as he listened to my stories, he told me that because my visions started coming to me from childhood and had continued throughout my lifetime, he found my experiences to be heartfelt and believed that I was receiving true inspiration. He also told me that I needed to write this book, as it was part of my individual spiritual path to do so. His encouragement played a great role in causing me to write *Cosmic Connection,* and to John Roberts I extend my thanks.

Unending love and gratitude go to my family, especially my loving and supportive husband, Marlowe. Anyone who is married to an author knows how difficult it can be at times. And being married to a writer who is also a psychic medium has to be a special challenge! Thanks go to my daughter, Jennifer, who keeps me supplied with Tinkerbell clothing, which I find to be uplifting since I had dreams of Tinkerbell years ago. Thanks to my son, Alan, for his enthusiasm about my writing and for frequently asking, "So how is the writing going, Mom?" And thanks to my daughter-in-law, Anita, who keeps me supplied with the Indian food I love so much. Many a night I was able to write when I might have instead been preparing dinner. Special thanks to my son-in-law, Constantine, for his incredible sense of humor, which always reminds me to look at the funny side of life. It goes without saying that my four grandchildren bring me the depth of joy that is essential to my spiritual development. Love to you, Greg, Natasha, Irina, and Angelina.

I express my deep gratitude to all of the authors whose books have been an important part of my spiritual journey and education. It is impossible to list all of these authors, but special thanks go to Deepak Chopra, Sri Aurobindo, the Mother, Satpreem, Wayne Dyer, Elaine Pagels, and Ira Progoff. Their contributions to my spiritual unfoldment have been enormous.

I give great thanks to the spiritual energy that guides me in my life and from which I have learned so much. Throughout my life, I have felt the presence of a power greater than myself. In my mature years, I have learned how to communicate more fully with this energy and receive guidance and inspiration.

About the Author

Photograph © Irene Downes/
Inspired Images

CAROLE LYNNE WAS QUITE HAPPY as founder of Singing for the Soul and Quality Performance Coaching for public speakers and performers. Little did she know that in mid-life, the world of spirit would let her know that she had the ability to communicate with the spirits of loved ones who had passed over. As those in spirit began to communicate with Carole Lynne, she knew that she was receiving an awesome gift and sacred responsibility. For years she studied both in the United States and Europe to learn how to use her gifts responsibly. She has become a popular psychic medium working in many countries. In this book, she reveals for the first time teachings from other entities known as "My Guidance" and "The Energy." Lynne is also author of the award-winning books *Consult Your Inner Psychic, How to Get a Good Reading from a Psychic Medium,* and *Heart and Sound.* She divides her time between Boston and Maui. Find Carole Lynne online at *www.carolelynnecosmicconnection.com.*

To Our Readers

WEISER BOOKS, an imprint of Red Wheel/Weiser, publishes books across the entire spectrum of occult and esoteric subjects. Our mission is to publish quality books that will make a difference in people's lives without advocating any one particular path or field of study. We value the integrity, originality, and depth of knowledge of our authors.

Our readers are our most important resource, and we appreciate your input, suggestions, and ideas about what you would like to see published. Please feel free to contact us, to request our latest book catalog, or to be added to our mailing list.

Red Wheel/Weiser, LLC
500 Third Street, Suite 230
San Francisco, CA 94107
www.redwheelweiser.com